ABOUT THE AUTHOR

Jack Aspinwall was born in the North. He has been connected with voluntary caring work for many years. He founded and motivated many projects for the care of the elderly and for those less fortunate in society. In 1979 he was elected to Parliament to represent the constituency of Kingswood near Bristol, and in 1983 the constituency of Wansdyke. Mr Aspinwall has travelled widely and has been inspired to continue his work in the literary world after visiting Third World countries. Many charities have benefited from the proceeds of his books and will continue to do so.

KINDLY SIT DOWN!

Best After-Dinner Stories from Both
Houses of Parliament

Compiled by Jack Aspinwall, MP

Illustrated by Timothy Jaques

CENTURY PUBLISHING

LONDON

Note to First Edition:
In the course of the production of this book there have been
a number of changes of Members' positions in the Houses of
Parliament. While every effort has been made to keep up with
these changes, it has, inevitably, not been possible to make all
the necessary alterations.

First published in Great Britain in 1983 and 1984
by Buchan & Enright, Publishers, Ltd
53 Fleet Street, London EC4Y 1BE

First published as a paperback in 1985
by Century Hutchinson Ltd,
Brookmount House,
62-65 Chandos Place, London WC2N 4NW

ISBN 0 7126 1031 6

Printed in Great Britain in 1985 by
The Guernsey Press Co. Ltd,
Guernsey, Channel Islands

FOREWORD
by
the Right Honourable
Margaret Thatcher, MP

I gladly welcome Jack Aspinwall's omnibus edition of his two earlier books of jokes and stories, culled from those in and around public life.

The two volumes have brought lots of life and laughter to many a stodgy meeting, and have raised many thousands of pounds for some excellent charitable causes. So for those in politics and elsewhere who have the wit to know that boredom is the great enemy, this omnibus has the wit to put that enemy to flight. I wish it the widest possible success and circulation.

July 1985

DEDICATION

To Brenda, my wife, who in thirty years of marriage has never lost her sense of humour, and has worked even harder than I have.

To Margaret Thatcher for writing the Foreword to this omnibus edition, and for her example and encouragement.

To Barbara and Madge for helping to make it all happen.

To all those wonderful friends and colleagues in and around Parliament who through their generosity provided the material for this omnibus version — after all, the favourite after-dinner story is a very much prized possession!

INTRODUCTION
Jack Aspinwall, MP

The omnibus edition of *Kindly Sit Down!* and *Hit Me Again! (I Can Still Hear The Swine)* will, I hope,bring you a great deal of fun and pleasure. I have many a quiet chuckle when I think of some of the stories.

There are many occasions in the House when a Member whispers in my ear and asks for a suitable story for a special event. I have jokes to suit many occasions and most have been tried out and tested too, and I duly receive a report back confirming my assessment!

The original idea for the books came when I was recovering from a compressed fracture of the spine after a sponsored parachute jump in aid of charity that for me had gone disastrously wrong, and I became determined to be successful at least at something. I thought of editing a book of after-dinner stories — the material to come from my excellent colleagues in Parliament (and others), all to raise funds for charity. This is what I have done and both the books became bestsellers, making large donations to charity possible.

Parliament is full of interesting characters who show great wit and humour from time to time, and the opportunities for their expression occur frequently and, I might add, are not limited to Members only. If I have helped to show people the humorous side of Parliament, then that cannot be a bad thing. The ability to laugh sometimes at ourselves has a chastening effect which, I am sure, in the end might help to bring some of us down to earth.

An example the other day certainly did! I was walking along a corridor in a not particularly well-lit part of the House with my wife Brenda, and coming towards us was a well-dressed coloured gentleman with an umbrella over his arm and a smile on his face. I was certain that I knew this gentleman — my mind flitted to Africa where I had recently been, and I thought that I had better say something. I called out, 'Good morning — how are you? Where have I seen you?', expecting to receive some information which would help me to recognise my smiling friend. My wife whispered to me hurriedly, 'He is the lift attendant'. I hastily explained my predicament and all three of us sent peals of laughter ringing through the corridors of power!

In an effort to promote improved overseas trade and jobs for one of my constituency businesses, a meeting was arranged between a trade attaché group from a foreign government and the chairman of a local company at the East India Club in London. I was standing just inside the impressive entrance waiting for my colleagues when I noticed Denis Thatcher there, whom I had met briefly on a couple of occasions. I went over and introduced myself as one of the Prime Minister's 'boys'. He was very pleasant and we chatted briefly until his friend arrived and he went into the dining-room for lunch. Eventually I settled down for a meal with my guests. Some time later Denis Thatcher came past my table, stopped, greeted us all, and said — 'Jack, how nice to see you again so soon.' He made my day!

Arriving in Rome by air from the Far East in the early hours of the morning, I took a bus from the airport to the centre of Rome, then a taxi to my hotel. The taxi driver was extremely friendly and helpful. When I arrived at the hotel he took the luggage out of the boot of his car, and I paid him and gave him a tip. He immediately shook my hand, patted me on the back and kissed me on both cheeks! This EEC business is being taken too far, I thought. Deeply embarrassed I went into the hotel, walked up the stairs, and got to thinking. I then realized that I had given the taxi driver £25.00 instead of £2.50, and also a tip to boot!

Shortly after Winston Churchill left the Conservatives and joined the Liberals, he took a young lady out to dinner. She looked up at him coquettishly and remarked with some audacity, 'There are two things I don't like about you, Mr Churchill.' 'And what are they?' 'Your new politics and your moustache.' 'My dear madam,' he replied suavely, 'pray do not disturb yourself — you are not likely to come in contact with either!'

It is said that Disraeli, when Prime Minister of England, was known particularly for his excellent memory. He was asked how he managed to remember all those names and never offend anyone by appearing not to recognise Members of Parliament on sight. The Prime Minister replied, 'When I meet a man whose name I cannot remember, I give myself two minutes: then if it is a hopeless case, I always say — "And how is the old complaint?" '

One of the guests at a fund-raising party in my new constituency of Wansdyke was a 94-year-old lady to whom I was introduced. She spoke softly and I didn't quite hear her name, and I asked her to repeat it. The remark she made certainly made me think, for she gently replied, 'When introductions take place the name you always hear is your own!'

After a long spell in hospital that followed my parachuting accident, when I sustained a fractured spine, I became an out-patient at a local hospital. One day I was sitting on a bench alongside an old lady wearing a surgical collar around her neck. We eventually got talking, and I asked her what was wrong with her. She replied she had fallen down the stairs and chipped a bone in her back. Inevitably came the question 'What happened to you?' I thought for a moment and told her that I had fallen out of an aeroplane. The old lady looked carefully around and then said, 'I think you have come to the wrong place. This is the Physiotherapy Department—the Psychiatric Wing is on the other side of the hospital!'

My wife, Brenda, was introduced to a colleague of mine in the Central Lobby of the House of Commons. After much hand-shaking and kisses on both cheeks, my colleague asked my wife how her feet were now? Somewhat indignantly, she replied that her feet were fine, and what did my friend mean? He replied very gracefully that he thought they might have been bruised when she fell down from heaven!

An ornithologist crossed a carrier pigeon with a woodpecker, producing a bird that would not only carry messages, but would also knock on doors when it arrived!

Lord Denning, PC, DL Master of the Rolls until 1982
This is a letter which I received from the International Students' House. I introduce it by saying that some people, even in London, do not know who the Master of the Rolls is:

Dear Lord Denning,
    I am an Indian citizen. I graduated in Mechanical

Engineering in the University of London and was awarded a Master of Science degree. I feel I have the necessary qualifications, motivation, energy, drive and personality to begin a successful career in an automobile industry. I will ever remain grateful to you if you would kindly help me to begin my professional career with your Company, the Rolls-Royce Motor Company ...

So he thought that I was either the Chairman of the Company or the driver of one of their cars.

Ron Dearing, CB Chairman, Post Office

The Post Office undoubtedly performs many social roles but seldom does it ever go as far as it did in a large sorting office a few days ago where a letter arrived addressed to 'God in Heaven'. Having sorted all the other letters, the postmen in the office gathered around in a group and one of them opened the letter.

Inside was a conventional note with the writer's home address in the top right hand corner (including the postcode of course). The postman read it out to his colleagues. It read:

Dear God. I am in desperate trouble and I need £30 to get out of it. If you can let me have £30 I promise to become a better Christian, to pray every night and to go to Church every Sunday.

The staff, in their usual warm-hearted way, had a collection and raised £12. They turned the money into notes, put them into an envelope, addressed it to the man and posted it again with a first class stamp.

The following night, at the same sorting office, the same staff saw another letter addressed to 'God in Heaven'. Once

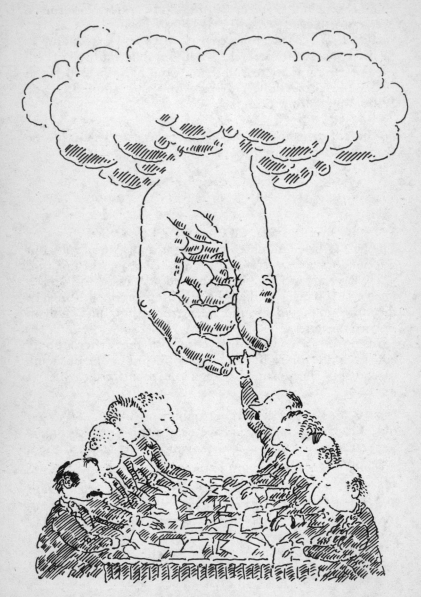

again, having done their job, they gathered round. The letter was opened and read to the group. It read:

Dear God. Thank you very much for the £12 you sent me. I did ask for £30. I did need £30. I have no doubt that you sent £30, and that those thieving so-and-sos in the Post Office took the rest.

Eric P. Cockeram, JP, MP

Picture two gates to Heaven, one with the notice: 'Queue here all men who are henpecked by their wives', the other carrying the notice: 'Queue here all men who are not henpecked by their wives'. St Peter arrived at the gates one morning to find a long queue of men trailing into the distance behind the former gate and one small insignificant looking man standing behind the second gate. On enquiring from him as to his qualifications for seeking entry through that gate, he replied, 'I really don't know, my wife told me to come and queue here.'

Lord Barber, PC, TD

At every meeting which the by-election candidate had held, his speech was ruined by a little old lady who followed him around. She always sat in the front row and, just as he was making his final remarks, would invariably shout out, 'If you were the Archangel Gabriel, I wouldn't vote for you!'

'If I were the Archangel Gabriel,' he replied, 'it is most unlikely that you would be living in my constituency!'

Lord Aberdare, PC

An English tourist, who rather fancied his meagre knowledge of French, went over on a day trip to Calais and had a meal in a restaurant. He found a fly in his soup and summoned the waiter by calling out a very Anglicised version of 'Garçon'. When the waiter arrived, he pointed at the fly floating in the soup and said repeatedly, 'Le mouch, le mouch!' The waiter with great dignity replied, 'Excusez-moi, Monsieur. C'est la mouche.' 'Good heavens,' said the diner, 'I must say, you Frenchmen have marvellous eyesight!'

Sir Philip de Zulueta, Kt

There is an American story about a petitioner before a US Internal Revenue Court who observed, 'As God is my Judge, I do not owe the tax assessed.' The Judge replied with commendable brevity, 'He is not, I am, you do.'

Lord Grey of Naunton, GCMG, GCVO, OBE

An Englishman, a Scotsman and an Irishman were cast away on a desert island. In that unpromising environment the myths of history were forgotten and they lived amicably, although restlessly, together. One day, rooting rather aimlessly in the sand, they came upon a metallic object which proved to be an ancient brass lamp. By rubbing the sand off, it produced the inevitable Genie. He said, 'I can give you fellows three wishes, that is, one each, fulfilment of which is guaranteed.'

The Englishman immediately wished that he be returned to his loving wife and family, and he left. The Scotsman said that he could not improve on the Englishman's wish, and he too vanished. After an anxious pause for consideration, the Irishman said, 'I shall be so lonely here without my two friends that I wish them back again.'

William Wormald

A man went into Harrods' vegetable department and was heard to have the following conversation:

CUSTOMER: 'Two avocados, please.'

SALESMAN: 'Yes, Sir, large or small?'

CUSTOMER: 'Large.'

SALESMAN: 'Thank you, Sir. That will be £4.50.'

CUSTOMER: '£4.50 for two! You know what you can do with them, don't you?'

SALESMAN: 'Yes, sir ... I'm sorry I cannot oblige you at the moment; I'm dealing with a complaint from a customer over the price of a pineapple ...'

The Duke of Bedford

Once, whilst speaking at a meeting, I was given a doubtful microphone so I asked, 'Can you hear me at the back?' The answer came, 'Yes,' and I replied, 'I am glad, for I was speaking somewhere the other day, and when I asked the same question, a lady at the back said, "No", and one sitting at the front got up and said, "I can – let me change places with you!" '

Lord Moyne, MA, FRSL

I know no after dinner stories, which is perhaps the reason that I have only spoken once after a dinner and was never asked to do so again!

Martin Stevens, JP, MP

A hairdresser and a Member of Parliament arrived in Heaven simultaneously. St Peter handed the MP his bicycle, the key to his council flat and a folder of luncheon vouchers. The new arrival was just moving away, quite contented, when he noticed the hairdresser being shown to his chauffeur-driven Rolls-Royce, into which a case of champagne was being loaded. The title deeds of his country estate were being carried by a secretary and St Peter was pointing out the spacious town house which had been allocated to him. The Member of Parliament said, 'I don't want to complain, but why is that other chap doing so well? After all I *was* an MP.' St Peter replied, 'Heaven is jam-packed with Members of Parliament – but he's the first hairdresser we've ever had.'

Lord Strauss, PC

'Your name?' asked St Peter at the gates of Heaven.

'Mary Smith,' replied the applicant.

'There are many Mary Smiths,' said St Peter. 'Can you identify yourself further? For instance, by your husband's last words. We have a full record of last words.'

'Certainly. They were, "Mary, if you are ever unfaithful to

my memory, I will turn in my grave".'

'Ah,' said St Peter, 'you must be the widow of the man we know as "revolving Smith".'

Major-General The Viscount Monckton of Brenchley, CB, OBE, MC, DL

On his way back from the Commons to his Club in St James's, F.E. Smith (later Lord Birkenhead) always called in at the Athenaeum to use the lavatory. He did this for some months, until somebody asked the Secretary if he was a member and it was discovered that he was not. The next time he arrived at the Club, the Secretary was standing ready to greet him, and asked him if he was a member.

'Oh,' replied F.E. Smith, 'is it also a club?'

Lord Brimelow, GCMG, OBE

Two Poles meet on the street.

'Have you heard the latest news?' asks one. 'The Russians have landed on the moon.'

'What? All of them?'

Lord Mancroft, KBE, TD

Some months ago I was rung up by the Chairman and Secretary of one of the Inns of Court Debating Societies, with which I have long been on friendly terms.

'Lord Mancroft,' they said, 'give us your advice. Do you know the Lord Chancellor, Lord Hailsham?'

'Yes, of course,' I said, 'Why?'

'Well,' they replied. 'Tell us quite frankly. Do you think he would be mortally offended if we were to ask him to step in at literally a minute's notice and take the place, at our annual dinner, of our guest of honour who's fallen sick?'

'Now steady on,' I said. 'Lord Hailsham is not only a Senior Cabinet Minister, he is also one of the most sought-after speakers in the country. It depends largely, doesn't it, upon the calibre of your stricken guest of honour. I mean, if you've succeeded in attracting to your table somebody outside the normal run of after-dinner speakers – the Ayahtollah Khomeini, for instance, or Miss Elizabeth Taylor, perhaps *that* might make a difference. Who is it?'

They mentioned the name of a Mr Bert Buggins, or somebody I'd never heard of in my life before.

'Good heavens,' I said, 'you can't do that to somebody of Lord Hailsham's calibre. He'll be mortally offended. Bitterly hurt.'

'Oh Lord Mancroft,' they said, 'how grateful we are to you for speaking so frankly. You've saved us from making fools of ourselves and dropping a dreadful brick.' Then, after a short pause, 'Lord Mancroft, I suppose *you* wouldn't care to come and make the speech for us?'

Martin Stevens, JP, MP

A Central European peasant was granted three wishes in exchange for sparing the life of a frog. He asked for great wealth, royal birth, and a beautiful wife. There was a flash of lightning and he came to, to find himself between silken sheets, in a four-poster bed under a royal coat-of-arms. A lovely girl, in bed beside him, took him into her arms. 'Get a move on, Franz Ferdinand,' she said. 'We are due in Sarajevo in twenty minutes.'

Sir Shuldham Redfern, KCVO, CMG

Some forty years ago, Mr Justice Norman Birkett was the Guest of Honour at a dinner in Toronto given by the Ontario Bar Association. The Chairman was the Canadian judge Mr Justice McCarthy, who introduced Birkett in a long and rather conventional speech. Birkett, one of the greatest of after-dinner speakers, began his reply as follows:

There is a legend among the Irish that when a child is born it is kissed by an angel. If the angel kisses it on its brow it will grow up to have great intellectual qualities. If the angel kisses it on its hands it will soon show unusual manual dexterity. If the angel kisses it on its feet it will become a swift runner and a good athlete. I don't know where the angel kissed Mr Justice McCarthy, but he certainly makes an excellent Chairman.

Sir John Osborn, MP

Quite often on public occasions, I have to explain that my name is John Osborn and that I neither write plays nor books. Frequently John Osborne's correspondence is muddled with mine and since I have entered Parliament we have had to exchange letters with each other on several occasions. But in 1957 I was on a business visit to the United States of America, well before I had given any serious thought to being a Member of Parliament.

My flight left late, and I drove through Broadway to my hotel noticing that *Look Back in Anger* was having its première that week. When I reached my hotel, it did not occur to me that the bellboys, porters and receptionists might be

16

aspiring actors and actresses. As my flight had left late, and as I had arrived after 7 o'clock, I learned to my chagrin that my reservation had been cancelled. I made some wry comment to the effect that this was a fine way to treat an Englishman on a visit to New York, but a sweet girl behind the reception counter said:

'Say, Mr Osborn, did you say you came from England?'

My reply was 'Yes'.

'Did you say your name was John Osborn?'

My reply was 'Yes'.

'Then you must be *the* John Osborne?'

Naturally my reply was 'Yes' – and I got a room immediately.

William Deedes, Editor, *Daily Telegraph*

Hark to the tale of Frederick Worms
Whose parents weren't on speaking terms;
So, when Fred wrote to Santa Claus,
He wrote in duplicate, because
One went to Dad and one to Mum,
Each asking for plutonium.

So Fred's father and his mother,
Without consulting one another,
Each sent a lump of largish size,
Intending it as a surprise.

These met in Frederick's stocking, and
Laid waste some ten square miles of land.
Learn from this tale of nuclear fission,
Not to mix science with superstition!

Lord Porritt, GCMG, GCVO, CBE

A junior Civil Servant went to the office of his senior with important papers and, after knocking and getting no reply, cautiously opened the door to find his Chief standing, with his hands behind his back, looking out of the windows onto Whitehall. The junior felt it wiser to retire quietly – but on being informed of the urgency of the message he carried, he returned an hour later, and again knocked on the door of the Chief's office. Still receiving no reply, he ventured in and cautiously made his presence known.

His Chief turned slowly and said, 'Quite extraordinary, Smithers, but I can now understand why this country doesn't prosper. I have been watching the workmen out there and they haven't done anything for the past hour!'

Neil Marten, PC, MP was conducting a group of his constituents around the Houses of Parliament when he came to a lobby of the House of Lords to be confronted by the Lord Chancellor, Viscount Hailsham, in all his regalia. The Chancellor immediately recognised him and called out, 'Neil!', and with that, the constituents – misinterpreting the call – fell down upon their knees.

Ian Lang, MP

A certain Scottish Labour MP, not noted for his assiduous attendance at the House of Commons, also had the reputation of being difficult to contact at home.

On one occasion, a Parliamentary colleague telephoned

him, to be greeted with:

'Hello, this is a recording. I am out at present on constituency business. Would you please leave your message after the tone and I will attend to it as soon as possible. Pip! Pip! Pip!'

'Hello. This is your Party Whip speaking. I wanted to let you know that there is an important vote in the House on a three-line whip, on Tuesday night, so I hope you will be there to support the party.'

'Oh, it's you, Hugh! Why didn't you say so? What can I do for you?'

Mrs Lynda Chalker, MP

So often one hears today that 'lack of communication' is the cause of the lack of understanding between those 'in authority' and those subject to such authority; e.g. that the clergy have nothing in common with those to whom they preach, and the politicians have nothing in common with those whom they punish.

I received a telephone call one day from the deputy governor of a prison, where I was a visiting magistrate, which stated that one of the prisoners had a complaint to make and insisted on seeing me. I duly visited the prison and listened to the complaint which the prisoner was making on behalf of himself and several others. I told him that whilst I considered the complaint to be serious and justified, I could not understand why he could not have waited until the next regular call of the visiting magistrate nor why he had insisted upon seeing me in particular.

He replied that he had discussed the matter with his fellow prisoners, and they all felt that the complaint should be made to me personally. I said that this was what I could not understand – why to me?

To this question he replied, in all seriousness, that they all took the view that their complaint would receive much greater consideration from me because, he said, 'we all think you are so much like one of us.'

I like to think that this was meant as a tribute. Or was it?

David Mellor, MP

A missionary was walking along a jungle path in Africa one day when he suddenly came face to face with a lion. Fearing that his last moments had come, the missionary fell to his knees and covered his face with his hands.

Seconds, it seemed almost like minutes, ticked away and nothing happened, and hope began to dawn in the missionary's breast. Gingerly, he pulled aside his fingers and peeped through. He was startled to see the lion, similarly on his knees with his paws covering his eyes.

The hope that had begun to dawn, swelled, and became real optimism. Then the lion pulled his paws aside, stared at the missionary and said, 'I don't know about you, mate, but I'm saying grace!'

Robert Rhodes James, MP

A favourite story of mine which used to be told by Mr Kruschev.

One freezing day in the Ukraine, there was a little boy walking through the woods, whistling. Suddenly, he saw a small bird with a broken wing, being chased by a hungry fox. The little boy picked up the bird, comforted it, and then looked for a warm and comfortable place where it could recover. At that moment, along came a horse and left a large deposit on the road. The little boy scooped a hole in the

deposit, put the little bird in it, and went away, whistling.

He was quite right. In the warm environment of the dung the little bird recovered, and put out his head and sang for joy. The hungry fox heard it, and ate the little bird.

The moral of this story is twofold: First, it is not always your enemies who put you in it, and secondly, if you are in it up to your neck, keep your mouth shut!

There is a moral here for all politicians!

Julian Amery, PC, MP

This story is based on a visit to the Military Hospital in Singapore by the Secretary of State for War. The setting is a ward with three corporals in it.

SECRETARY OF STATE FOR WAR: 'Corporal Tomkins, what's the matter with you?'

CORPORAL TOMKINS: 'VD, Sir.'

SEC. OF STATE FOR WAR: 'I am sorry about that. Wouldn't have expected it from a non-commissioned officer with your experience. What's the cure?'

TOMKINS: 'They gives me a brush, they gives me some ointment and they tells me to paint the affected part.'

SEC. OF STATE FOR WAR: 'What's your ambition?'

TOMKINS: 'Get well, so I can go back to Malaya and kill some terrorists.'

SEC. OF STATE FOR WAR: 'Good man.'

The Secretary of State for War then moves to the next bed and remarks:

'Corporal Smith, what's the matter with you?'

CORPORAL SMITH: 'Piles, Sir.'

SEC. OF STATE FOR WAR: 'I believe it's very distressing.'

SMITH: 'Yes Sir, very distressing.'

SEC. OF STATE FOR WAR: 'What's the treatment?'

SMITH: 'They gives me a brush, they gives me some ointment, and tells me to paint the affected part.'

SEC. OF STATE FOR WAR: 'What's your ambition?'

SMITH: 'Get well, Sir, and get back to the Regiment as soon as possible.'

SEC. OF STATE FOR WAR: 'Good man.'

The Secretary of State for War goes to the next bed and asks:

'Corporal Brown, what's the matter with you?'

CORPORAL BROWN, (faintly): 'Laryngitis.'

SEC. OF STATE FOR WAR: 'What did you say?'

BROWN: 'Laryngitis, Sir.'

SEC. OF STATE FOR WAR: 'Very tiresome for you. What's the treatment?'

BROWN: 'They gives me a brush, they gives me some ointment, and they tells me to paint the affected part.'

SEC. OF STATE FOR WAR: 'What's your ambition?'

BROWN: 'To get the brush before the other two.'

John Carlisle, MP

On the occasion before the England *v* Wales rugby match at Twickenham, I made two requests to one Speaker. The first was for an Adjournment Debate later that week, and the second for tickets for the match. His reply was as follows:

'The first request is within my power and I can accommodate, the second, however, is beyond my jurisdiction, but I can assure you of one thing: if England beats Wales at Twickenham on Saturday, you will not be called to speak before Easter!'

John Corrie, MP

An old lady who was lonely bought two parrots. She was not

sure which was male and which was female.

'Ah,' said the pet shop owner, 'it's easy to tell the difference. Parrots make love every morning: the answer is to cover the cage, creep in first thing, and whip off the cover; you can pick out the male bird as he always shuts his eyes and has a rest.'

The old lady did this and, sure enough, was able to pick out the male, but to ensure that she knew him in future she cut out a little white collar and put it round his neck.

All went well until two weeks later when the Vicar called to tea. The male parrot looked up, saw him and squawked, 'Tough luck, you were caught at it as well, I see!'

Toby Jessel, MP

A man who thought he was a dog was sent to a psychiatrist who said, 'This is very serious – we had better have a talk about this. Please go over there, lie down on that sofa and relax; to which the man replied, 'Sorry, but I am not allowed on sofas.'

Lord Porrit, PC, GCMG, GCVO, CBE

A junior Civil Servant found a 'Top Secret' document on his desk, read it, initialled it and sent it out to his Chief. The latter, furious at this presumption on his junior's part, called him in and dressed him down, saying, 'You will delete your initials and initial the deletion!'

John Lee, MP

In 1975 the Nelson and Colne Constituency Conservative Association's Selection Committee were interviewing possible candidates to take on the sitting Labour Member of Parliament, Douglas Hoyle, at the General Election.

One question to a young aspirant from the South of England was put by a Selection Committee member with a strong Lancashire accent: 'What are you going to do about Doug 'oyle?'

The aspiring candidate, nervously fingering his tie and looking for guidance from the Chairman, said, 'I ... I wasn't sure there *was* any oil in this constituency.'

Percy Grieve, QC, MP

From a platform in Hyde Park, at Speaker's Corner, a left-wing agitator was haranguing the crowd on the benefits to be derived from full-blooded Socialism. 'When the dawn of freedom comes,' he said, turning to a little man in a cloth cap on the edge of the crowd, 'you will be riding down Park Lane in a Rolls-Royce car, with a top hat on your head.'

'Beg pardon, Guv,' said the little man, 'I couldn't see meself in a top 'at. I'd rather stick to me old titfer.'

'Very well, then,' said the orator. 'When the dawn of freedom comes, my friend, you will be riding down Park Lane in a Rolls-Royce car, wearing you own old titfer.'

'Beg pardon, Guv.' said the little man. 'Couldn't really see meself in a Rolls-Royce. Think I'd be far better on me old bike.'

'Look here,' said the orator. 'When the dawn of freedom comes, you'll do what you're bloody well told.'

Michael Jopling, PC, MP

A Member of Parliament was giving prizes away at a Girls' School's Speech Day. Afterwards the Head Mistress asked how much he wanted to cover his expenses, which he naturally refused. To this, the Head Mistress replied: 'Oh! That is generous. It will allow us to put the money we had for your expenses into a special fund we have.'

The MP did not like to ask what the special little fund was for but, in the end, his curiosity got the better of his good manners, and he did ask. The Head Mistress replied: 'Oh! It is a special little fund so that we can afford a rather better speaker next year!'

Malcolm Rifkind, MP

In the 1930s there was an old Scots Provost of a small burgh in Scotland, who, having been recently elected to his office, had to preside over his first civic banquet. He was told that his first responsibility would be to propose the Loyal Toast to His Majesty King George V. Having never had to give such a Toast before, nor having heard one proposed, the Provost spent many days preparing a lengthy speech extolling the many virtues of His Majesty, which he intended to use in the Toast he was to make.

Fortunately, he showed the proposed lengthy speech to the Town Clerk, who was aghast at the kind of speech that had been prepared and who informed the Provost that when one was proposing the Loyal Toast, one was merely expected to propose the health of His Majesty and then sit down.

The Provost was somewhat annoyed and disconcerted at this advice, but he felt that he had no alternative but to accept it. Accordingly, on the night in question, at the appropriate time he rose and addressed the assembled guests in the following fashion: 'Ladies and Gentlemen, I wish to propose the Toast to His Majesty King George V and the Town Clerk tells me the less I say about him the better!'

Stephen Hastings, MC, MP

A surgeon, an anaesthetist, an architect and a politician were discussing which of their professions was the most ancient. The surgeon claimed that it must be his since the resection of Adam's rib was well documented and constituted a major operation. The anaesthetist said that if that was so, then there was no doubt that a deep sleep had been necessary beforehand and that therefore his practice preceded the surgeon's. 'Maybe,' said the architect, 'but before all that happened, it was the task of the architect of the universe to arrange the stars in their courses and to produce order from chaos.'

The politician looked knowingly at the three of them and said, 'And who do you suppose created the chaos?'

Sir Anthony Royle, KCMG, MP

This story is about a knight who returned to his castle late in the evening in a state of total disarray, with dented armour, his face bleeding, his horse crippled, and the knight himself about to fall off the limping animal.

'What has befallen you, goodly knight?' asked the lord of the castle.

'Sire, I have been working for you, robbing, raping and pillaging your enemies in the West.'

'You have what?' cried the lord. 'I do not have any enemies in the West.'

'Oh,' said the knight. 'I think you do now.'

Lord Glendevon, PC

Two horses met when out for a walk, and one said to the other 'I know your pace but I can't put a mane to it.'

Lord Renton, PC, KBE, TD, QC

Dr W.G. Grace had a son who was a master at Oundle. When they were both invited to play cricket for the Masters against the 1st XI hundreds of people came to see the great man play, and when he went in to bat there was tremendous applause. The school fast bowler, however, bowled him out first ball – and an awful groan was heard all round the ground.

On his way back to the pavilion WG said to the boy: 'Young man! You see all those people – they didn't come here to see you bowl!'

Lord McFadzean, KT

There was a teetotal preacher who once ended his vigorous sermon with the plea that: 'All liquor should be thrown into the river', only to go on and announce as the last hymn: 'Shall we gather at the river'!

Sir Hugh Fraser, PC, MBE, MP

A young Minister was sent to Moscow and found whilst he was there that he had to attend a dinner and thereafter make a speech. He decided to surprise everyone by making the speech in Russian.

He set about learning his speech but, since time was short, he could only learn the Russian phonetically.

The speech he had prepared was a short one but as he was on his way to make it, he realised that he did not know how to say 'Ladies and Gentlemen'. He stopped the car and looked about him and there, in front of him, was the very public place he was looking for. He set off once again for the dinner.

As he started to speak in Russian he found that he did not get the delighted applause he had expected – more a deathly silence. The rest of the speech seemed to go better and he did receive a polite appreciation at the end of it.

Afterwards he asked one of his colleagues what had gone wrong. The colleague replied: 'The speech was excellent. It might just have been that you started off "Male and female urinals"!'

Reg Prentice, PC, JP, MP

Many reasons have been given by people as to why they should have crossed the floor from one political party to another (I should know!), but this story gives one that is slightly unorthodox:

Tom and Harry had been active Conservatives for many years, working together in the same branch. When Tom was taken ill, Harry visited him and was astonished to hear the statement, 'I have just decided to join the Labour Party.'

'For goodness' sake, why?' asked Harry. 'You have been a "True Blue" Tory all your life. Why change now?'

'Well, I am not feeling at all well. I do not like the way the doctor is looking at me. I feel I may not have long to live. And if someone is going to die, I would rather it was one of those so-and-sos, not one of us!'

Robin Leigh-Pemberton, Governor of the Bank of England, FRSA, CBIM

A well-to-do country lady formed the ambition to establish a fine pedigree herd of beef cattle. Local opinion, including that of the Ministry of Agriculture, doubted her ability to do this and she was well aware of these doubts. When the herd had been assembled, she invited the Ministry Officer to come and inspect it, and he was compelled to admit that it was indeed a very fine herd. 'But,' he continued, 'if I had a herd of thirty head, I would have twenty-nine cows and one bull and not, like you, fifteen cows and fifteen bulls.'

'Yes, I know,' she replied, 'but that's a man's point of view.'

Baroness Hornsby-Smith, PC, DBE, FRSA

When Under-Secretary of State at the Home Office, I was due to visit Remand Homes and Borstals in the West Country. I was met at Exeter by a police car to complete my cross-country schedule. On proceeding to Plymouth, I was met by the Chief Constable in his car and he led the way to what had been an old mansion. On parade and gazing through the French windows were thirty 'naughty' girls.

The Chief Constable leapt out of his car and joined me,

while my police driver opened the door and the girls goggled. That it might be courtesy never entered their heads – it could only be *custody* – an awe-struck voice uttered: 'Cor blimey, she must be an 'ot one – 2 police cars and 3 cops to bring 'er in.'

Sir John Tilney, Kt, TD, JP Chairman, Airey Neave Memorial Trust

I like shorter stories, the shorter the quip the better. For instance, the story of the prisoner in the dock who said after being sentenced, 'Me Lud, I swear I am innocent, but I will never do it again!'

Lord Beswick, PC

The motivating power of professional pride should not be under-estimated. Consider for example the following case.

A Corporation in a certain totalitarian country was adjudged by the appropriate court to have failed the nation. The Chairman, Finance Director, and Engineering Director, were each sentenced to death by guillotine.

On the appointed day, before a great crowd, the Chairman put his head on the block and the lever was pulled, but the blade did not fall. The law of the land forbade a second try and the Chairman walked away a free man.

The Finance Director went next. Again the lever was pulled, and again, the blade failed to fall and the Finance Director also was freed.

Then came their remaining colleague. The Engineering Director put his head upon the block; as the lever was about

34

to be pulled he looked up and called out, 'Wait a minute. I can see what's wrong.'

Hugh Cubbitt, CBE, FRICS, JP, DL, FRSA

A newspaper editor wrote a swingeingly critical article about his local council in which he claimed that '... half the Councillors are crooks ...' After strong remonstrance and threat of libel action, he amended on publication to '... half the Councillors are *not* crooks....'

The Duke of Norfolk, CB, CBE, MC, DL

I have often found it hard to explain who I am when answering the telephone, and on one occasion, having said, on lifting up the receiver, 'Duke of Norfolk', I got the spontaneous reponse: 'What's that, a pub?'

Sir Shuldham Redfern, KCVO, CMG

A firm of insurance brokers put up a new and very modern office building in the City and wanted to have on the outside five plaques, each of which would represent some aspect of insurance. They therefore sent for Epstein, explained what they wanted and left it to him to submit drawings of appropriate designs.

In due course the drawings arrived. The first was of a man in bed with his wife, the second of a man in bed with his fiancée, the third of a man in bed with his secretary, the fourth of a man in bed with a lady of easy virtue and the fifth of a man in bed alone. When they saw these drawings the members of the Board were furious. They sent for Epstein and said that there must be some misunderstanding, for not one of these drawings appeared to have anything to do with insurance.

'On the contrary', said Epstein. 'Each of these drawings does, as you requested, represent some aspect of insurance. For instance, the first, of a man and wife, is Legal and General. The second, of a man and his fiancée, is Mutual Trust. The third, of a man and his secretary, is Employer's Liability, and the fourth, of a man and a lady of easy virtue, is Commercial Union.'

'What about the fifth, a man alone?' said the Managing Director.

'Oh that,' said Epstein, 'is obviously Prudential.'

Lord Blake, FBA, JP

The Chairman of a meeting, as Chairmen sometimes do, introduced the guest speaker at inordinate length, reciting all major and most minor details of his career. At last he finished and said, 'I will now ask Lord Birkenhead to give his Address.' Lord Birkenhead replied, '32 Grosvenor Gardens, SW1,' and walked out of the hall.

Tom Benyon, MP

A man rang his local District Council and spoke to the Ratings Officer.

'How much extra do I pay for building a stable block, a huge barn and a greenhouse?'

'£400 p.a. extra.'

'Excellent, I have just pulled them down!'

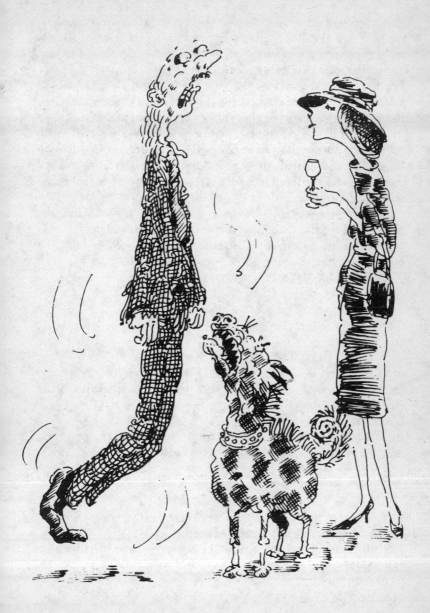

Barry Henderson, MP

Having rescued a mongrel from the Cat and Dog Home we found we were often asked her breed. At first we didn't like to be too crudely direct about her very mixed ancestry.

As she was called Sheba, for a day or two we had been answering the usual question by calling her an 'Ethiopian Moon Hound', until my wife giving this answer at a cocktail party got the reply, 'That's interesting, we were in Ethiopia last month and didn't see any of them.'

Next week I was in Dundee and a large and cheerful lady, enchanted by the dog, asked the usual question, to which I replied 'I'm afraid she is quite unique.' She said, 'A euneekie, I havna come across one of them afore.'

We no longer bother with euphemisms!

The Earl of Waldegrave, KG, GCVO, TD, DL

Q. Name a well known husband and wife in the Bible?
A. Dan and Beersheba.
Q. No.
A. I forgot, Sir ... of course, they weren't properly married ... what about Sodom and Gomorrah?

Sir James Hanson, Kt

The difference between political beliefs:
SOCIALISM: You have two cows, and you give one to your neighbour.

COMMUNISM: You have two cows, the government takes both of them and gives you the milk.

BUREAUCRACY: You have two cows, the government takes both of them, shoots one of them, milks the other and pours the milk down the drain.

CAPITALISM: You have two cows, you sell one of them and buy a bull.

The Viscount Trenchard, MC

'I can clearly discern a light at the end of the tunnel.'

Private Secretary: 'Are you sure, Sir, that it's not an engine coming the other way?'

Lord Home of the Hirsel, PC, KT

A man who was losing his memory consulted a specialist.

SPECIALIST: 'When did this begin?'

PATIENT: 'When did what begin?'

Lord Stuart

The elephant looked at the mouse and said, 'Why are you so small?' The mouse replied, 'Oh, dear, I have not been very well recently.'

Lord Harmar-Nicholls, MEP, JP

A mother flea giving guidance on Life to her three daughters said, 'Always have a worthy watchword and adhere to it. Mine has always been "perserverance".

'When I was a young and beautiful flea like you are now, I lived on a church hassock. One day I heard that an Archbishop was coming to our church and I made up my mind that I would taste the Archbishop.

'On the great day I hid in the porch and when he arrived I jumped on his hand, but he brushed me off. I persevered and followed him down the aisle and jumped on his neck, again he brushed me off. Still I persevered and followed him to the altar and jumped behind his ear, and it was there, my children, that, as a result of my perseverance, I tasted my first Archbishop; but what is more, it was there that I met your dear father.'

Ivan Lawrence, QC, MP

I once attended a meeting where the Toastmaster announced the main speaker thus:

'My Lords, Ladies and Gentlemen, pray for the silence of your Member of Parliament.'

Lord Carr of Hadley, PC, CH

An ageing Bishop found himself increasingly unable to cease from wondering whether there were any golf courses in Heaven. He even put the question into his prayers.

One day, while meditating, he received a direct message

from above: 'Don't worry,' the Heavenly messenger said. 'There are plenty of the most wonderful golf courses, they are always in perfect condition, and never have any wind or rain to put you off your game, and, of course, there is a great choice of the nicest people to play with.'

'Oh, that is wonderful news,' said the Bishop.

'Yes,' replied the messenger, 'but now for the bad news. You are down to play in a match on Saturday!'

Lord Duncan-Sandys, PC, CH

I am told that the Dean of Windsor once asked King George V what he would like him to preach about on Sunday, to which the King replied, 'About ten minutes.'

D.R.W. Silk, JP, MA, The Warden, Radley College

A Bishop was struggling through a Series 3 service with a microphone which seemed not to be working. He turned to the Dean who was beside him, and, tapping the microphone, he whispered to the Dean, 'There is something wrong with this thing.' Back came the instant response of the large congregation, 'And also with you.'

The Viscount Rochdale, OBE, TD, DL

An eminent writer of prose and poetry had become very run down, so he went to his doctor to ask what he should do. The doctor immediately told him to go away into the country for a while, for a change and rest.

He followed the doctor's advice and went to a little

country hotel. When the time came for him to leave, the landlord realised that to have something written personally in his Visitors Book by such an eminent writer would be a great boost. He therefore asked his guest if he would write something. The latter was rather irritated, but eventually was persuaded to contribute, and this he did as follows:

'My doctor sent me here for a change and rest,
The waiter took the change and the landlord took the rest!

The Hon. William Waldegrave, MP
Two lunatics visit the House of Commons.

They watch happily as Members boo, shout and catcall. They feel more and more at home as order papers are waved, and old gentlemen in knee breeches and swords lead away the Member for Boltover.

Suddenly a bell rings, and everyone scurries away into the lobbies. 'Ah,' says one lunatic to the other, 'someone has escaped.'

Lord Caccia, GCMG, GCVO
There are many tales ascribed to Nasrudin in the Near and Middle East. One, recorded amongst others, in the *Pleasantries of the Incredible Mullah*, describes how he stood up in the market place and started to address the throng.

'O people! Do you want knowledge without difficulties, truth without falsehood, attainment without effort, progress without sacrifice?'

Very soon a large crowd gathered; everyone shouting, 'Yes, yes.'

42

'Excellent,' said the Mullah, 'I only wanted to know. You may rely upon me to tell you all about it, if I ever discover any such thing.'

J. Allan Stewart, MP

There are countless stories about the attitude of the English to the Scots and vice-versa. My favourite concerns an election meeting in England where the speaker was being mercilessly heckled by an immigrant from north of the border.

Stung by the remarks about his integrity and patriotism, the speaker began his peroration, 'Mr Chairman, I am an Englishman, I have always been proud to be an Englishman, and I venture to suggest I always shall be proud to be an Englishman.'

'Man, man,' came the sorrowful question, 'dae ye huv nae ambition at all?'

Eamon Kennedy, Ambassador, Irish Embassy

Diplomats know that the timing of their démarches is all-important. It is said that when Machiavelli was on his deathbed he was visited by a humble priest who wished to offer the last rites.

'Wake up, Machiavelli,' he said, 'I'm here to give you the last rites. Tell me – do you renounce the devil?'

Machiavelli's eyes were open now and he peered at the holy man.

'Do you renounce the devil?' asked the priest again.

'Renounce him?' replied Machiavelli. 'Surely you don't really think this would be the right time to antagonise him?'

The Viscount Norwich, FRSL

James McNeill Whistler commissioned a house – the White House, Chelsea – from his architect friend, E.W. Godwin. Some years later, when Whistler was compelled by poverty to leave the house, he put up a plaque over the door. It read: 'Except the Lord build the house, their labour is but lost that build it. E.W. Godwin, FSA, built this one.'

Sir Kenneth Lewis, DL, MP

Moses went up the mountain to negotiate The Commandments with the Lord on behalf of the children of Israel.

But Moses first discussed with the shop stewards at the bottom of the mountain, everything which, it was thought, the Lord might require in the Commandments.

Moses returned after some time and said he had done his best to get a deal.

Moses said, 'The Lord wanted fifteen commandments – I tried to get this reduced to eight – so, we settled on ten and I am sorry to have to report that number seven (about adultery) which you Comrades wanted out, has had to stay in!'

Lord McFadzean, KT

An opening when one has been rather forced to make a speech:

'As I stand up to speak I am vividly reminded of the man who built himself a grand house with an ultra-large swimming pool. Having invited many friends to a big party round the swimming pool and plied them with drinks, he then invited any of them to swim in the pool, notifying them that there was a live alligator in it but that anyone who did go in and get out safely could have half his estate or the hand of his younger daughter in marriage.

Naturally, nothing much happened until one man was seen swimming madly for the steps hotly pursued by the alligator. When he had reached safety, the host, in congratulating him, asked him which of his offers he wanted: half his property or the hand of his younger daughter in marriage.

'Neither,' spluttered the swimmer furiously. 'I only want one thing and that is to find the b——r who shoved me in.'

An opening sentence, when one feels totally inadequate for the particular occasion:

The story of the two cows munching contentedly in a meadow when down the adjacent country lane came an ultra-modern milk tanker with the words protruding from its gleaming cylinder, 'This milk is Standardised, Pasteurised and Homogenised with Vitamin D added.' Said one cow to another while shaking its head sadly: 'It does make you feel so totally inadequate.'

An appropriate story in an overseas country, when there are foreigners there who do understand English fairly well and you are going to give part of your speech in the language of the country you are in. Drift in to such part of your speech with due apologies and the memory of the foreigner who was trying desperately to impress his British audience with his knowledge of English and said: 'You think I know damned nothing but I can assure you I know damned all.'

Lord Simon of Glaisdale, PC, DL

At a recent dinner my name appeared next on the toast list. The Chairman rose and said, 'I now call on our little northern nightingale.' I was a little surprised, but then I'd failed to notice a musical interlude. Just as I was opening my mouth, a soprano, who'd taken her place at my elbow, burst into song. When she had finished the Chairman rose again and said, 'That concludes the part of the evening devoted to your entertainment – I now call on Mr Simon.'

Sir Anthony Royle, KCMG, MP

Boring speakers remind one of the famous old politician who having talked interminably and boringly about himself, turned to his companion and said, 'I have talked about myself long enough. Let's talk about you. What do you think of me?'

Sir Monty Finniston, Kt, BSc, PhD, FRS, FRSE

'Lord, thank you for the food we are about to eat, and for the company gathered here this evening, all of whom hold responsible positions in industry and commerce. Guide us in our actions and decisions in that they are taken in the best interests of those for whom we are responsible and not purely for the advancement of ourselves as individuals. When it comes to my time to speak, Lord, fill my mouth with worthwhile stuff and nudge me when I have said enough.'

Lord Wade, DL, MA, LLB

Chairman: We are very grateful to Lord Wade for coming to speak to us at such short notice. I can assure him that we would have been very willing to make do with a less distinguished speaker, but we couldn't find one!

The Viscount Mountgarret

A man who was a good friend of an eminent member of the Royal Yacht Squadron was invited to give a post prandial talk at the Squadron's Annual Dinner. The Dinner was for men only, and when the time came for the speech to be made, the man rose to his feet and said, 'Gentlemen, it is a very great honour to be invited to speak to you this evening, but I am at a loss to know exactly what to talk to you about. It is pointless my talking to you about matters concerning sailing, as I am not half as experienced as all of you, but I do know a considerable amount about sex – and I propose to speak to you about that.' And so he did.

The following morning his wife was up at her usual punctual hour, with her husband still sleeping off the effects of a rather jovial evening the night before. Outside, she happened to meet somebody who had been at the dinner. 'Oh,' she said, 'I'm so delighted to see you – I've been dying to know how Willie got on last night. I was sound asleep when he got back, and he hasn't surfaced yet. Do tell me what happened.'

'Oh,' her acquaintance replied, 'he was an absolutely roaring success. He was frightfully funny, and we all thoroughly enjoyed ourselves.'

'Oh, I'm so glad,' she said, 'you see I was terribly worried about him. He's only done it three times. The first time he was violently sick. The second time his hat blew off, and the third time he got all tangled up in the sheets!'

Lord Maybray-King, PC, DCL, PhD, FKC
At a meeting the speaker started by saying, 'I'm going to talk to you about Yale University – Y-A-L-E – Yale: Y for Youth, A for Ambition, L for Loyalty and E for Endeavour'; and he spoke for half an hour on each.

He later said to a friend, 'Did you like my speech?'

'Yes,' came the reply, 'but it's a good job it wasn't on the Massachusetts Institute of Technology!'

The Hon. Peter Brooke, MP
Letter from a schoolgirl,
'Dear Aunt,
The school did *Hamlet* last week. Most of the parents had seen it before, but they laughed just the same.'

The Hon. Archie Hamilton, MP
I am always rather touched by the story of the speaker who finds himself in much the same position as the third husband-to-be of Brigitte Bardot, a man some years younger than his would-be bride. He was asked how he viewed his forthcoming marriage, and replied, 'I know what I am supposed to do, but it is a question of how to make it more interesting.'

51

Tom Benyon, MP

A man went to stay at a hotel in Workington. On the second day he rang room service: 'Please send me some tepid coffee, some soggy toast, a raw egg and some warm orange juice.'

'Sir, I am afraid we don't provide that sort of breakfast, we are a 4-star Hotel.'

'Why not? You did yesterday!'

Lord Maybray-King, PC, DCL, PhD, FKC

A man died and went to Heaven. He knocked at the door and it was opened by Satan. The man was astonished. 'Don't worry,' said Satan. 'We've gone comprehensive.'

Lord Lloyd of Dolobran, MBE, DL

A bishop who was not renowned for the brevity of his sermons, visited one of the churches in his Diocese. When he arrived, he was not best pleased to find a total congregation of about ten people including the choir.

After the service was over, he said to the Vicar, 'That was a very small congregation we had this evening, did you not tell your parishioners that I was coming?'

'No,' said the Vicar, 'but I'm afraid that it must have leaked out!'

Sir Shuldham Redfern, KCVO, CMG

A Bishop was once giving a lecture to a class of small boys on the subject of Moral Courage. At the end of the lecture he said: 'Now can any boy give me a good example of Moral Courage?' A boy put up his hand and said: 'Yes, Sir, I can. There were twelve boys in a dormitory and when they went to bed eleven of them undressed and jumped into bed, but one of them knelt down and said his prayers first. That showed Moral Courage.'

'A very good example,' said the Bishop. 'Can you give me another example?'

The same little boy put up his hand and said he could give another example. 'If there were a dormitory in which there were twelve Bishops, and, when they went to bed eleven of them knelt down and said their prayers but the twelfth jumped into bed without saying his prayers, *that* would also be an example of Moral Courage.'

Sir Russell Fairgrieve, CBE, TD, JP, MP

The dinner was a 'somewhat dry' affair, and a 'somewhat dry' guest, although not on the official list of speakers, suddenly got up and proposed, 'absent friends, coupled with the name of the wine waiter'.

John Heddle, MP

Sir Thomas Beecham was travelling south, having conducted the Hallé Orchestra, in a first-class non-smoking compartment (before the days of railway nationalisation). At Stockport he was joined by a buxom lady who promptly lit up a cigarette.

She asked Sir Thomas Beecham: 'I hope you don't mind if I smoke,' to which the great composer replied, 'Not if you don't mind my being sick!'

'Sir,' she replied, 'I'll have you know that I am one of the directors' wives,' to which Sr TB replied 'Madam, I don't mind if you are the director's *only* wife!'

Eamon Kennedy, Ambassador, Irish Embassy

There was a charming old Irishman living out his last days in a home for the aged in Dublin. To the delight and curiosity of the nurses he seemed to spend every last moment learning the lovely old Gaelic language.

'And why are you spending every moment learning the Irish?' they asked him wonderingly.

'Well, it's because when I go to Heaven all the saints will surely be talking the Gaelic,' he said.

'Well now,' said one of the nurses in fun, 'aren't you the presumptuous old man! Supposing you didn't go up? Supposing you went down, the other way?'

'Not to worry,' said the old man serenely. 'Sure, haven't I got the grand store of English!'

Field-Marshal Lord Harding of Petherton, GCB, CBE, DSO, MC

I was complaining to an old fellow West Countryman about having to make after dinner speeches for which, unlike another field-marshal, now sadly deceased, I have little liking and less aptitude. He gave me the following advice: 'Get out of it if you possibly can. If you can't, then stand up straight, speak out loud, and sit down quick!

Sir Kenneth Lewis, DL, MP

A doctor said to his patient who had been back many times, 'I confess, I do not know what is the matter with you, you must have Alice.'

'What's Alice?' asked the patient.

'I don't know,' said the doctor, 'but Christopher Robin went down with it.'

Michael Colvin, MP

The Vicar was having a bad cricket season. He was a member of the team because the cricket field was Church property. All efforts to drop him for this key match were to no avail. His record for the season was dreadful: batting average 3, bowling average infinity and, luckily, no-one kept a tally of the boundaries let through, or the catches dropped.

The Captain placed him at long-on, knowing that the visiting team's opening pair were a stodgy couple and that

the Vicar would be safely out of the way on the boundary behind the bowler.

Alas, contrary to all expectations, the batsman opened his shoulders to the first ball and sent it high into the air over the bowler's head; almost certainly a boundary.

The Vicar was off like lightning. Dashing down the boundary, he flung himself full length and caught the ball six inches from the ground with one hand.

The spectators roared; the Vicar tossed the ball into the air, caught it, rolled over, and the crowd roared with laughter. He bounced it off his nose, and tossed it in the air again. Then, suddenly, hearing the sound of pounding feet, he looked up to see the bowler thundering towards him.

'Throw it in, you bloody fool,' he shouted. 'It was a no-ball, and they've already run eight!'

Lord Maybray-King, PC, DCL, PhD, FKC

Three young Americans were asked who they would like to meet in the next world.

The first said: 'Abraham Lincoln, the greatest of all Americans.'

The second said: 'Robert E. Lee, the noble General of the South.'

The third one was then asked who he would like to meet and he said: 'Brigitte Bardot.'

'But, she's not dead.'

'Neither am I!'

Peter Viggers, MP

Her Brittanic Majesty's Ambassador to Washington was

telephoned by an American he had met at a diplomatic reception. 'I'm telephoning to ask what you would like for Christmas,' said the American.

The Ambassador was embarrassed. He had only met the American once, knew him to be a hugely rich newspaper tycoon, and felt it quite wrong to accept a present from him. He politely demurred, 'Nothing at all, really nothing.'

The American persisted, 'I will be deeply disappointed if you won't tell me. Just name what you are hoping for at Christmas.'

The Ambassador thought quickly. The best way out of the predicament appeared to be a diplomatic compromise: 'Well, if you insist, perhaps a small box of crystallised fruit … that would be very nice … thank you very much.'

The Ambassador thought nothing more of the matter until a few weeks later, shortly before Christmas, m a member of his staff silently entered the Ambassador's room, laid an item on the desk and tactfully withdrew.

The item was a newspaper cutting from one of the journals owned by the American. It read: 'At this time of goodwill we have asked the official representatives of other nations to express their wishes for Christmas and the New Year. The French Ambassador hopes for progress towards disarmament through the Strategic Arms Limitation Talks; the German Ambassador hopes that the Brandt Commission Report will lead to the relief of poverty in the Third World … and the British Ambassador hopes for a small box of crystallised fruit.'

Lord Hooson, QC

An irate female member of an audience suddenly shrieked at Lloyd George: 'If I was your wife I would give you poison,' to which the great man immediately replied, with excessive courtesy, 'Madam, had I the extreme misfortune to be your husband, I'd take it.'

Lord Wolfenden, Kt, CBE

Some years after the end of the Second World War Winston Churchill was enjoying a relaxed evening with a group of intimate friends. One of them pointed out the paradox that the countries which had lost the war, Germany and Japan, were the most prosperous in the world, while the victors, Britain and the United States, seemed to be in an increasingly poor state. 'And what,' enquired Churchill, 'do you propose we should do about it?'

'Well,' said another mischievously, 'we might fight another war and lose it.' Long pause.

'Um,' said the Old Man, 'and whom do you propose we should fight it against?'

'I thought,' came the reply, 'that we might declare war on the United States.' Longer pause.

'Um, well,' rumbled the Great Leader. 'Yes, but, you see, we wouldn't lose.'

Lord Boyd-Carpenter, PC, DL

This is a true story and relates to my grandfather, the late Doctor William Boyd-Carpenter, Bishop of Ripon and Clerk of the Closet to Queen Victoria.

He was summoned one day to Windsor to advise the Queen. It had been discovered that the cobbler who repaired the shoes of the Royal Household at Windsor was an atheist. The question was whether, this having been discovered, he could retain his job.

'Well,' said my grandfather, 'Your Majesty can hardly expect a cobbler to believe in the immortality of the soul.' There was a pause during which it looked as if it was not only the cobbler's job which was in jeopardy. Then the Great Lady gave a hearty laugh and two competent professionals retained their employment.

Lord Orr-Ewing, OBE

When I started in the political field and I was nursing a constituency, I took every opportunity of accepting invitations to speak. I received one from a lunatic asylum and, with some trepidation, accepted it as I felt it would be good practice.

After I had been going for three minutes, a man at the back stood up and shouted: 'Rotten.' I took another run at the sentence with the same result, and when it happened the third time I turned to the Governor of the asylum, who was by my side, and said: 'Shall I go on?'

He replied: 'Do go on. We have had this man here for twenty years and it is the first time I have heard him talk any sense at all!'

Basil de Ferranti, MEP

One evening, having made a speech, a young man came up to the rostrum and said, within everybody's hearing, that mine was the lousiest speech that he had ever heard. The Chairman of the meeting, seeking to defuse the situation, made matters worse by turning to me and saying, 'Oh, Mr de Ferranti, you mustn't mind that young man. All he ever does is to repeat what everyone else is saying.'

Leslie Porter, Chairman, Tesco Stores (Holdings) Ltd

Just after the last World War two German ex-officers decided to go to Paris for the weekend. They knew that very attractive ladies gathered during the cocktail hour at the George V Hotel, and thus headed straight there. They agreed that they would only speak English, for fear of ruining their chances.

They entered the lounge of the hotel, called the waiter over and in beautiful English one said: 'Two Martinis, please, waiter.' 'Dry?' asked the waiter, to which one of them immediately answered: 'Nein, zwei.'

Lord Balfour of Inchrye, PC, MC

There was a Bishop of portly dimensions who was very conscious of the dignity of his office. Whenever the Bishop was asked to speak at a dinner, loving his food very much, he would look at the menu to see whether it was worthy of his cloth. If the Bishop thought this not to be the case then he would start his grace: 'Lord, we are not worthy of these, the least of thy mercies.' On the other hand, if he thought it worthy of his position he would start: 'Bountiful Jehovah'.

Tim Brinton, MP

On two occasions I have had meetings interrupted by animals, the non-parliamentary kind. The first time was during a Conservative branch party in Sussex. I was addressing the gathering across a pond in a farmyard when, having just made a rousing Tory point, a lusty cockerel gave loud voice from the barn. The laughter took nearly two minutes to fade.

The second time was whilst opening a fête to raise funds for the Association. I was urging one and all to give generously when I was interrupted by a great deal of barking, as two rival groups of dogs clashed. My comment on both occasions was that people should take no notice, as it was probably only the local Liberal party.

Lord Hooson, QC

During a pro-Boer meeting which was extremely rowdy and restless, a man in the audience threw a cabbage at Lloyd George. He caught it, and, turning it round and looking closely at it, said, 'Ladies and Gentlemen, just as I feared, one of my opponents has lost his head.'

Lord Leverhulme, TD,

A benevolent old gentleman coming home one day, saw, right in front of his house, an overturned load of hay blocking up the road. A small boy was trying to get the hay back into the cart. The gentleman said to the boy, 'Have you to put all that hay back into the cart?'

'Yes, Sir,' said the boy.

'Have you had your dinner?' asked the gentleman.

'No, Sir.'

'Well then, come inside and have your dinner. You will work better for it.'

'I don't think my father would like it,' replied the boy.

'Oh, your father would not mind. Why should he mind

your having a good dinner?'

After dinner he said to the boy, 'Now just you have a walk round my garden and then you will be ready for your work.'

'Please, Sir, I don't think my father would like it.'

'Oh, your father won't mind. He will be glad for you to do it. You have a walk round.' And the boy did. On his returning to the house, the gentleman said, 'Now I have a nice book here. Just look at a few pictures and then you will be ready for your work.'

'But please, Sir, I don't think my father would like it.'

'It's all right, I am sure your father will not mind. But what makes you keep saying you do not think your father would like it?'

'Please, Sir, he's under the hay!'

Dr Immanuel Jakobovits, Chief Rabbi

Three men, having been doomed by their doctors to die within three months, were asked how they would spend the time left to them. The Scotsman answered that he would cheerfully squander his savings on all the pleasures he had previously denied himself. The Frenchman spoke of the utter abandon with which he would dine and wine to his heart's content. And the Jew simply said, 'I would look for another doctor to get a second opinion.'

Richard Body, MP

A former Member of Parliament for the Isle of Wight was not a little taken aback by his reception at the Annual Dinner of one of the Conservative Women's Branches in his constituency – he had begun by saying, 'How good it is to see so many old Cowes faces.'

The Hon. Alan Clark, MP

During the 1922 election Lady Astor was contesting the Sutton Division of Plymouth. She chose, in characteristic and autocratic defiance of the Representation of the People Act, to canvass in the company of the dashing and handsome Admiral of the Fleet, Earl Beatty, DSC, who accompanied her in full dress uniform.

At that time Lady Astor was at the very pinnacle of her physical beauty and she too affected expensive raiment, her grey eyes only thinly concealed by a silk veil, etc. etc. They must have made a most handsome, indeed overpowering, couple.

Lady Astor knocked on the door of a humble house in the Efford district. It opened a few inches. An elderly, but not unworldly face showed itself.

'Good afternoon, I am Lady Astor, your Member of ...'.

The door opened and the crone spoke: 'That's right, just along the corridor, under the stairs.'

'No, I don't think you understand. I am Lady Astor, your Member of Parliament, and I am asking for your support in the General Election, which is to be held next Thursday.'

'I don't know nothing about that. My husband just says when the lady comes along with the sailor show 'em to the room under the stairs.'

Reginald Eyre, MP

One day in ancient Rome a Christian was put into the lion pit to await the arrival of the hungry lions. A great beast entered the pit and made his way towards the Christian, licking his lips. The Christian moved quietly to the side of the lion and whispered a few words in his ear. At once the lion turned and slunk away out of the pit. A second lion appeared roaring hungrily but, again, the Christian whispered in his ear and the lion turned and walked disconsolately away. A third lion appeared. Again, the Christian whispered in his ear with the same result.

Nero, who was presiding over the festivities, was fascinated and asked for the Christian to be brought before him. 'Christian, if you will tell me what words you whispered into the ears of those lions, I will give you your freedom.'

'Caesar,' said the Christian, 'it was quite simple. I merely told him that after dinner he would, of course, be expected to make a speech.'

Lord McFadzean, KT

There is the story of the slightly intoxicated policeman who stopped a car and demanded to know if it was licensed. 'Of course it is,' said the irate driver.

'Thank God for that,' said the policeman, 'I'll have a gin and tonic.'

John Page, MP, Chairman, Inter-Parliamentary Union

This story was told by the Leader of a Chinese Parliamentary Delegation, Mr Hao Deqing, at a Parliamentary luncheon given in his honour by the Inter-Parliamentary Union.

This is an old story of a Chinese gentleman who was visiting, for a meal, a friend who was renowned for his meanness. When he was leaving his host took him to the front door, where the guest said, 'Where is the threshold board on your front door?'

The host replied, 'I have never had one here'; to which

the guest said, 'Oh, how silly of me. I must have had too much to drink ... before I arrived!'

Eldon Griffiths, MP

When your Chairman asked me to volunteer to speak tonight he advised me to say just a few words, but like most members of the House of Commons I have never quite known what a few words really means! I was, however, given a definition of this phrase the other night while dining with a Federal Judge in the great American state of Georgia where, as we finished our meal, there was a knocking on the door and there was admitted a most attractive young man with what is known in these parts as a 'Georgia peach'. The young couple asked if the Judge would marry them, to which he replied that unfortunately they would have to wait a few days. Listening unhappily to this, the young man replied, 'But, Sir, could you not say a few words, just to see us through the weekend!'

Sir Angus Maude, PC, TD, MP

A Member of Parliament fell ill and went to hospital. For ten days, he received no letters, no visits, not even a grape. On the tenth day he received a letter on his Association writing paper from his agent which read as follows:

Dear George,
At last night's meeting of the Divisional Council I was instructed to inform you that a Resolution was passed expressing the deepest sympathy with you in your illness and wishing you a speedy recovery. This motion was carried by 28 votes to 19, with 10 abstentions.

Sir Bernard Braine, DL, MP

A fellow parliamentarian, not exactly the most popular of men, was reading *The Times* at breakfast one morning when his eye alighted on the obituary column. There, to his astonishment, was his own obituary. There was no mistake about it – the newspaper thought that he was dead and, what made matters worse, did not seem to think much of him and his life's work.

He went to the telephone and rang a friend – he still had one left – and asked him if he had *The Times*. 'Yes,' replied his friend, recognising his voice, 'I'm reading it now'; and then, after one of those awkward pauses one sometimes experiences in an embarrassing conversation, he enquired, 'By the way, where are you telephoning from?'

Odette (Mrs Geoffrey Hallowes, GC, MBE, Légion d'Honneur)

When my husband attended his school Old Boys' Dinner, I always wondered what he and his friends talked about and did. I was therefore delighted, and honoured, when some years ago a friend asked me to be Guest of Honour at his Old Boys' Dinner.

I sat on the right of the Headmaster, and when he asked me if I was prepared to say a few words at the end of dinner, I moved my head too quickly and my contact lens fell in my soup.

I cannot see with my other eye and am therefore quite blind without the lens, and although I had prepared a short speech, I knew that, even if I could find my contact lens, I would be unable to put it back in my eye. Somehow I managed to retrieve it, slip it into my napkin and then

quickly into my bag. To this day I cannot remember what I said, but everyone seemed to be satisfied and happy, even if it was an all-male occasion with a female Guest of Honour for the first time.

After dinner I met many of the Old Boys; to the consternation of my hosts and my husband, when the youngest Old Boy, aged about eighteen, was introduced to me, he asked how old I was. When I told him, he recovered quickly, having seen the shock in the eyes of the other Old Boys, and partially redeemed himself in their eyes when he said, 'If I could take you out for the evening, I would be very proud.'

It showed he had been to the right school, but my husband never quite got over it!

John Heddle, MP

Travelling back from the hustings in Manchester during a General Election campaign, earlier this century, the great F.E. Smith (later Lord Birkenhead) found himself sharing a railway carriage with the legendary Keir Hardie.

Keir Hardie (obviously after a heavy night!) thought that he should strike up a conversation with F.E. and said, 'Cor blimey, Sir, I've got an 'ell of an 'ead', to which F.E. replied, 'My dear fellow – what you need is an aspirate!'

Sir Derek Walker-Smith, QC, MP

In proposing the election of Mr Speaker Thomas in the House of Commons, I told this story of the conversation between a former Ministerial colleague of his and a doctor:

Minister: 'There are two sorts of doctor – the young and

experimental, who kill you off, and the old and traditional, who leave you to die.'

Doctor: 'Yes, Minister, and there are two sorts of politician – those who are dead, and those who ought to be.'

Neil Macfarlane, MP

An eleven-year-old boy was sitting an end of school year examination. The question was asked: 'What is electricity?' After much thought and frequent gazing through the open window, he wrote, 'I did know, but I've forgotten.' When the paper arrived on the desk of the examination marker he penned in the margin, 'Only two people know about electricity – God who can't tell us ... and Tompkins, who has forgotten.'

John Langford Holt, MP

The Chaplain was giving an address to a detachment of soldiers who were about to be dispatched to the front. He ended his address with these immortal words: '... and now God go with you – I will go with you as far as the station.'

Cyril D. Townsend, MP

An elderly Peer was forced to attend a major debate in the House of Lords facing downwards. A colleague commiserated with him but the elderly Peer replied, 'I can assure you, Sir, I have heard some of the nicest things ever said to me in this position.'

71

Sir Philip Goodhart, MP

In the latter part of 1956, I was visiting Somalia as correspondent of the *Sunday Times*. Our Consul-General in Mogadishu, who was reputed to be the greatest living expert on the Somali language and was the author of the first Somali dictionary, arranged for me to go and see the new Prime Minister.

I arrived rather early at the Government Building, and was for once swiftly escorted through the various layers of attendants. The door of the Prime Minister's office was thrown open. I was ushered in, and found myself in the middle of the second meeting of the new Somali Cabinet.

I sat down in a chair at the end of the table, and the Cabinet looked at me expectantly. It was plain that I was expected to say something, and so, slowly and loudly, I asked, 'What is your economic policy?'

This provoked an animated discussion lasting for almost three-quarters of an hour. It was perhaps the first time they had discussed their economic policy. At last a man who I presume was their Chancellor of the Exchequer turned to me with a beaming smile and said, 'It is to discover oil!'

After I left Somalia I wrote a rather superior and cynical article about basing one's national economic policy on the discovery of oil. I had not then imagined that within twenty-five years it would become my own country's policy as well.

Hamish Gray, PC, MP

The oil industry attracted a number of Southern Scots into my Highland constituency of Ross and Cromarty. One such family enjoying a Sunday stroll in the country was

bombarded with questions from their 11-year-old son.
'Hey, Father, what is that four-legged beast called?'
'I'm not sure, laddie,' was the reply.
'Hey, Father, what is the name of that big hill?'
'I am not sure, laddie,' his father repeated.
'Hey, Father, what is the name of that river?'
'I cannot be sure, laddie,' came the answer.
'Now look, Father, you dinna mind me asking all these questions, do ye?'
'Of course not, laddie, if ye dinna ask, you will never learn.'

Sir Geoffrey Howe, PC, QC, Kt, MP
A British businessman had been invited to address a gathering of Japanese tycoons. He knew something of their customs, and particularly that they were a very courteous people. So, on rising to his feet, he bowed deeply to the assembled company. This gesture was greeted with an immense and enthusiastic cheer.

The businessman was so pleased by the response that he bowed to his audience a second time. This time the response was one of sullen, stony hostile silence.

The British businessman turned to his Japanese chairman and said, 'What have I done wrong?'

'These chaps don't like long speeches,' replied his host.

Delwyn Williams, MP
I was in a taxi going round Trafalgar Square when, in front of the taxi driver and myself, a TR7 sports car tried to cut in on a rather large bus. 'Cor blimey, Guv'nor, look at that,'

said the irate taxi driver. 'They shouldn't be allowed on our roads.' Inevitably a collision occurred which added to the taxi driver's wrath. 'Now they are holding us up,' he exclaimed. As we got level, it appeared that the two drivers were both coloured gentleman and were engaged in a slanging match. My taxi driver wound down the window and shouted out, 'Driver. Bloody driver,' and eventually one of the coloured men looked up. 'Why don't you both go back then?' he shouted. Thinking he was an irate member of the National Front I sought to placate him by saying, 'Yes, why not send them all back then.' To my chagrin he turned round and said, 'No, what I meant, Sir, was why don't they both reverse their vehicles, that way they will cause less damage.' At which, thank heavens, we both had a good laugh and carried on.

Roger Moate, MP

In thanking you for the splendid dinner tonight, might I say how much better it was than on another occasion when the speaker, having been asked if he had enjoyed his meal, replied:

'If the soup had been as warm as the wine,
And if the wine had been as old as the chicken,
And if the chicken had been as plump and as tender as the waitress,
And if she had been as willing as the elderly dowager sitting next to me,
Then it would have been an excellent meal.'

Ray Whitney, OBE, MP

This is a three-nation story. This time, an Englishman, a Frenchman and a Russian are arguing about what is the most pleasurable experience in life.

The Englishman begins by describing a lovely Sunday summer morning. He rises late, has a leisurely breakfast, just in time to stroll down to the pub for opening time. After several pints with his friends, he returns to a well-cooked lunch of roast lamb and mint sauce with new potatoes and fresh green peas from his garden. He then stretches out for a carefree post-prandial snooze. That, for him, is one of the most pleasurable experiences in life.

'Pouf!' exclaims the Frenchman. 'You English are so unromantic. For me, it is to take a pretty girl, with my wallet full, to my favourite nightclub in Paris, lots of French food, good champagne and soft lights. Then I take her back to my flat for the most pleasurable experience in life.'

'You decadent Westerners do not know that you are born,' says the Russian. 'Let me tell you what real pleasure is. You go to bed at, say, eleven o'clock. At about four in the morning, there is a loud and angry knock at the door of your flat. "Open up, open up," screams someone from outside the door. "Who is it?" you say. "It is the secret police. We have come for Ivan Ivanovich." My friends, easily the most pleasurable experience in life is when you are able to say, "Ivan Ivanovich lives next door." '

Kenneth Warren, MP

A noble Lord espied a hang-glider through the windows of his study and called to his faithful retainer, 'Carruthers, bring me my best pair of Purdeys.' Carruthers duly trundled forward, handed the guns to his Lordship who then went onto the terrace and gave the object in the sky all four barrels. 'Did you get it, My Lord?' the butler asked. 'No,' replied the ageing Peer, 'but I certainly winged it – got it to drop the poor devil it had in its talons.'

Giles Shaw, MP

The Archdeacon had attended the Rotary Club Annual Dinner and was departing relatively late at night in a somewhat merry condition. He passed the entry to an imposing block of flats where lists of cards were to be seen alongside bell pushes. The top name caught his attention. It read, 'St Paul'. With a reverential twinkle, he pressed the bell, despite the lateness of the hour. After a long delay an elderly gentleman, wrapped in a purple dressing-gown, opened the door.

'Is your name Paul?' asked our reverend friend.

'Yes. What on earth do you want at this time of night?' was the reply.

'I just wanted to congratulate you on your letter to the Ephesians,' slurred our respondent.

At which the door was slammed in the caller's face and the Canon tottered off into the night.

Five minutes later he was back, pressing the bell vigorously. The door was opened again, by a more irate version of the gentleman in the purple dressing-gown.

'And what do you want now?' he said.

'Sorry to trouble you,' said our friend, 'but I just wanted to know – did you ever get a reply?'

Cyril D. Townsend, MP

A few years ago Jim Prior was trying to reassure an audience which had expressed its concern about the unemployment figures. He pointed out that the Government had taken certain measures and there was bound to be a delay before the results were felt. He went on to use an agricultural illustration: 'If you put a bull in amongst the cows you do not expect immediate results.' At this a red-faced farmer from the back of the hall was heard to comment, 'No, Sir, but at least the cows look happy.'

Sir Peter Emery, MP

The first man to reach the planet Venus stepped out of his spacecraft to be welcomed by the most beautiful woman he'd ever seen: she had a marvellous figure, long blonde hair and aquiline features. He was amazed; not at her great beauty, nor that when she said, 'Welcome, man from the earth,' that she spoke in English, but, that with all this perfect beauty, she stood thirteen feet tall, her delightful proportions towering over him. Therefore when she turned and asked, 'Shall I take you to my leader?' his only response could be, 'Take me to a ladder, I'll see your leader later.'

John Spence, MP

A school inspector asked a class, 'Who blew down the Walls of Jericho?' One of the pupils, a lad called Billy Green, replied, promptly, 'Please, Sir, it wasn't me.'

The inspector was amazed at this show of ignorance and

brought the matter up in the headmaster's study at the end of his visit. 'Do you know,' he said, 'I asked the class who blew down the walls of Jericho and young Billy Green said that it wasn't him.'

The headmaster said, 'Billy Green, eh? Well, I must say that I've always found the lad to be honest and trustworthy, and if he says that it wasn't him, then it wasn't him!'

The inspector left the school without further comment, but lost no time in reporting the full sequence of events to the Ministry of Education in a written report. In due course, he received the following reply:

Dear Sir,
Reference the Walls of Jericho, this is a matter for the Ministry of Works and your letter has been sent to them for their attention.

Neil Thorne, OBE, TD, MP

During the course of the last General Election a young Conservative canvasser arrived at the gate of a recently purchased council house to find the gate closed securely with wire. Undaunted, he squeezed between the privet hedge and the gate post, walked up the path and rang the bell. On looking back towards the gate he noticed, to his horror, his footprints in the newly laid concrete path. Hearing a noise approaching the door he realised that it was too late to retreat and, upon the door being opened by the elector, thought it wisest to announce that he was calling on behalf of the Liberal candidate to seek support in the forthcoming General Election, before carrying out a hasty, strategic withdrawal.

Baron Snoy et d'Oppuers, KBE

The building of Europe came to a deadlock after the vote of the French Assembly on 30 August 1954, which rejected the Paris Treaty on the European Defence Community. It was difficult to imagine then how it would be possible to get it started again.

However, early in 1955, the Benelux countries envisaged a new move, which was called the 'Relance Européenne'. Together, they produced a cautious draft presenting a range of suggestions. The matter had to be submitted to the Council of Ministers of the Coal and Steel Community. But a meeting was difficult to convene – the diaries of the Ministers of Foreign Affairs were too full!

After a great number of consultations, one date only was found to be convenient – 1 June 1955 – but the Italian Minister, Martino, could not at that time leave Sicily, where he was waging an electoral campaign for the Assembly of the region. So, the condition of any ministerial meeting was that it should be held in Sicily. Happily, the other Ministers agreed.

There had been no international encounter in Sicily since the days of Frederic II Hohenstaufen, and nobody knew where the necessary facilities could be found. The only spot where accommodation could be sufficient was Taormina, but the Ministers objected that a conference at Taormina would never be taken seriously. Thus, we took the map of Sicily and found a little town not too near, not too far from Taormina, where it was possible to organise a meeting in the town hall and where we had a relatively easy road to Taormina – this was Messina.

The six national delegations arrived at the Hotel San Domenico in Taormina in a pleasant mood – the Whitsun holiday was just over and many a delegate had enjoyed relaxing in the beautiful resorts of southern Italy and Sicily.

The Belgian delegation, headed by P.-H. Spaak, arrived just at the same minute as the French, which was led by President Pinay, and I remember greeting the French Minister and Ambassador Wormser, together with a gentleman whom I had never met and who happened to be the senior alderman of the city of Saint-Chamond.

The formal meeting in Messina was to be held the next day at 4 p.m. The Sicilian temperature being what it is in early summer, good work could only be done late in the afternoon. We could thus enjoy a pleasant morning without too many duties. At 3 o'clock, the official cars escorted by carabinieri raised a cloud of dust on the road to Messina, and there we listened respectfully to speeches delivered by our superiors. On the second day of meetings, the Chairman, Luxembourg Minister Bech, who was anxious to finish early, turned to me at 6 p.m. and said, 'You have heard the speeches delivered by the members of the Council, now, it is necessary to draft the conclusions of the meetings and would you kindly summon the Ambassadors to a drafting committee. The Ministers will go back to Taormina where you will submit your draft to us, later in the evening.'

Being an obedient Civil Servant, I complied with these instructions, but after thirty minutes, the drafting committee was led to conclude that there had not been a clear understanding between the Ministers and that the kind words which had been exchanged were not sufficient to reach an agreement. We decided to go back to Taormina and report to the Ministers.

I found them sitting on the stone benches of the Greek theatre where the Rome Ballet was to produce dances in the unforgettable surroundings of a proud past. The stars and the moon were shining and the night was bright. I reported to Chairman Bech and explained that we needed a new ministerial meeting. He made such a gesture of despair that I said, 'Why not immediately? Perhaps after the ballet.' He replied, 'You forget that at midnight we are all invited by the

Italian Government to a dinner party in the San Domenico with all these charming ballerinas.' I answered, 'Well, Mr Chairman, the meeting could be held after the dinner, then.'

And that is what happened. The true Conference of Messina was held at Taormina, on 3 June, between 2 and 4 a.m. and it was serious business, with a lively debate and tremendous conclusions. The result was a communiqué full of substance, which was the starting point of two years of negotiations leading to the signing of the Rome Treaty on 25 March 1957.

I was so happy that I stood on the hotel balcony to enjoy the sunrise on Mount Etna, and called Spaak to share this unforgettable moment. The birds were singing and he joined them with an enthusiastic, 'Il Sole Mio'! Then we heard a window open above us and President Pinay's voice shouting: 'Can't you let people get some sleep?'

And that was how the European adventure began!

Lady Burnett

This is a story told to me by a very old friend, concerning an encounter he had with a local crofter on the Isle of Mull.

The visitor said, watching the crofter painting the outside of his house with a very small paint brush, 'Why do you not use a larger paint brush – it would be quicker.'

The crofter replied after a few minutes, 'Aye, but there is no twice the work to do.'

Lord Porritt, GCMG, GCVO, CBE

At a Veteran's Reunion that took place annually in Chicago, a Chinaman and a Jew used to meet regularly and became good friends. Despite enjoying each other's company, they always seemed to end up quarrelling.

On one occasion the Jew said to the Chinaman at the end of their argument, 'Well, anyway it was your people that were responsible for Pearl Harbor!'

The Chinaman, duly incensed, replied, 'That was the Japanese not the Chinese'; to which the Jew replied, 'Oh, well, Chinese, Vietnamese, Japanese – they're all the same to me!'

A year later the same sort of thing occurred and the Chinaman finished the argument by saying, 'Well it was your people that were reponsible for the *Titanic* disaster, wasn't it'; to which the Jew replied furiously, 'The Jews had nothing to do with it!'

The Chinaman replied, 'Well, Sternberg, Rosenberg, Iceberg – they're all much the same aren't they?'

Sir Anthony Kershaw, MC, MP

At a public meeting, a man was called upon to speak in place of Winston Churchill. He started by modestly saying that he could not understand why the choice should have fallen on him, except, perhaps, that it was because he had been a member of the Tory Party for even longer than Winston Churchill, though not, of course, so often.

Anthony Grant, MP

Whips are totally misrepresented in the eyes of the public. Far from being harsh, flinty men, who bully nervous MPs into Lobbies against their deeply held consciences, Whips are men of supreme tact, diplomacy, and persuasion. This is

well illustrated by the following example.

One night, or rather early morning, a Whip had to assemble all his MPs for a vital division in the House. He telephoned one who was in bed asleep with his wife. The wife answered the telephone. 'It is the Whip's office here. There is an urgent vote in the House – will you please ask your husband to come back and vote.' Without putting the telephone down she said, nudging her recumbent husband. 'It's the Whips. They want you to go back to the House.' In a sleepy but loud voice the MP said, 'Tell 'em I'm not here!' 'He's not here,' repeated the wife. 'Well, Madam,' the Whip said in a deadpan tone, 'will you please tell the gentleman who is in bed with you to come back and vote!'

Lord James Douglas-Hamilton, MA, LLB, MP

At the Coronation, the man in charge of the celebrations in London wrote to the Commissioner of the Royal Canadian Mounted Police, drawing his attention to the fact that the Mounted Police contingent would be riding through streets in London, lined by troops, many of whom would be wearing Bearskins, and that horses have a great aversion to Bearskins. The writer suggested that the Mounted Police horses therefore be familiarised with Bearskins before they came.

He got a letter back from the Commissioner of the Royal Canadian Mounted Police, thanking him for his courtesy and thoughtfulness, and saying that there was no problem, because the horses of the Mounties were used to bearskins, with the bears inside them!

Cyril D. Townsend, MP

When a former Pope asked the jazz trumpeter, Louis Armstrong, if he had produced any children, Armstrong replied that, no, he hadn't yet, but that he and Mrs Armstrong were having a lot of fun trying.

Vivian Bendall, MP

A young lady came to see a Member of Parliament at one of his surgeries (a Councillor also being present) and in common with other constituents started her long tale of woe. It should be mentioned at this stage that this story is in no way intended to mock this young lady, nor, indeed, to jest about any problem brought to the attention of the MP by a constituent. The MP thinks, however, that the young lady in question would join with him in finding some humour in her sad case.

She had, sadly, been slightly disfigured on the 'upper part of her anatomy' following cosmetic surgery, and she wanted to consult him as to whether she could take any legal action in order to be recompensed. During the interview the young lady produced, from a brown paper bag, an array of photographs which depicted her plight in full. One question did spring to the MP's mind during the interview – who took the photos? – but in the circumstances he refrained from enquiring. However, his curiosity was soon satisfied as the answer was offered quite casually: 'Of course, I had the photos taken at one of those little booths, at a station, where you can get passport photos taken.' The mind boggles at the thought of a cold, windy winter's day and a young lady braving the elements displaying all to the world with the little flimsy curtain flapping in the breeze!

Ian Stewart, MP

A sign seen above a chemist shop:
'We Dispense with Efficiency'.

Nicholas Baker, MP

A British businessman was travelling with a South American airline on an aeroplane which had two pilots.

The first pilot decided to take a stroll into the cabin to talk to the passengers, leaving his co-pilot in charge of the aeroplane. The co-pilot was suddenly caught short and, leaving the aeroplane controls fixed on automatic pilot, he went into the passengers' part of the plane to the lavatory.

Just at that moment the anti-hijack device, which causes the door between the pilot's cabin and the passengers' compartment to shut automatically and stay locked, came into operation and the door clanked shut.

The British businessman and the rest of the passengers then had the unusual experience of seeing two pilots using axes to break down the door to get back to the controls of the plane.

Ivor Stanbrook, MP

A man, after he got on a train, discovered that it was a non-stop to Sevenoaks and would not be stopping at Orpington. He managed to persuade the train staff to arrange with the driver, unofficially, to slow down, as the train passed through Orpington Station, to a speed at which he could safely jump off. When the time came he opened the carriage door, stepped out and ran with the train a few yards only to be grabbed by a passenger holding a door open in a following coach. He was pulled in. 'My goodness,' said the passenger, 'didn't you know this train doesn't stop at Orpington? It was lucky I saw you running for it!'

Hugh Dykes, MP

A senior politician was on an official visit to one of the newly independent African republics and on landing at a remote rural airstrip, he was invited by the Chiefs to address the assembled natives. He went through the usual ritual phrases – 'marvellous to be here' – 'wonderful country' – 'challenge of independence' – and was happy to note that, at the end of each sentence and paragraph of his oration, the enthusiastic natives shouted out, 'Umbula, Umbula!'

He concluded his speech to yet more outbursts of 'Umbula, Umbula,' and was then driven away to inspect a new farm.

As he was going through the cattle pens with the farm manager, he was very dismayed when the manager said to him, 'Be careful where you step, there is a lot of *umbula* about from the cows.'

Peter Hordern, MP

An Australian came to Britain to see his family, and caught a train from Victoria to Chichester in order to visit an elderly aunt who lived there. He bought a first-class ticket and

boarded the train. However, it was the middle of the summer and the train was absolutely packed. He walked along the corridor and eventually saw a first-class carriage with an old lady sitting in the corner and a Pekingese dog on the next seat. So the Australian entered the carriage and asked her very politely if she would mind if her Pekingese sat on her lap while he sat on the seat. She said, 'Certainly not. My dog is going to sit on this seat and you will have to go and find somewhere else.' The Australian walked across the carriage, opened the top window, picked up the Pekingese and threw it out. There was a startled hush and a gentleman sitting in the opposite corner looked over the top of his glasses and his copy of *The Times* and said, 'You know, you Aussies are all the same, you come over here, you murder our language and then you go and throw the wrong bitch out of the window.'

Robin Squire, MP

A well-known vet was telephoned after midnight by an elderly lady who lived nearby. She complained that, at the bottom of her garden, a dog and a bitch were mating noisily. The vet listened to the complaint and then said, 'Madam, do you know what time it is?' to which the lady replied, 'Well, yes, it's half past midnight.' 'Well why don't you tell them that one of them is wanted on the telephone?' said the vet. 'Will that stop them?' asked the lady. 'Well, it stopped me,' he replied.

Victor Goodhew, MP

The 18th century essayist, Joseph Addison, having been

elected to Parliament, rose one day to make his Maiden Speech. Like most other Members in a similar position he was extremely nervous and began by saying, 'Mr Speaker, Sir, I conceive ...' He paused and started again, saying, 'I conceive, Mr Speaker, Sir ...' A sympathetic Member murmured, 'Hear, Hear.' Taking a deep breath, he started once more and said, 'Mr Speaker, Sir, I conceive ...' and, unable to find another word, he sat down, completely lost.

The next Member called by Mr Speaker started, 'Mr Speaker, Sir, the Hon. Member who has just resumed his seat has conceived three times and brought forth nothing.'

Peter Bottomley, MP

During my by-election in 1975, my elderly grandmother came down to help me. I thought that she would be able to persuade people of her own age to consider voting for me, so I rang up the matron of a local old people's home to ask if I could bring my grandmother round. The reply was, 'Even if you get elected and become a Very Important Person, we would not be able to take your grandmother for at least three years, because there is a long waiting list.'

William Benyon, DL, MP

There was once a man whose wife died in India. On receiving the sad news, he asked for her to be embalmed and returned to England. When he opened the coffin he was surpised to find, instead of his wife, a general in full dress uniform.

In response to a frantic telegram, he received the following reply: 'Wife buried with full military honours, you may keep the general.'

John Butcher, MP
A definition of tact: The ability to see others as they see themselves.

Peter Temple-Morris, MP
A complicated legal action, after much argument, eventually found its way up to the Court of Appeal. For the third and final day of the hearing, the client had to leave on important business and requested that the result be sent to him by telegram. He won the case and it was decided that a suitable telegram should contain the immortal phrase, and that phrase only: 'Justice has been done.' The telegram was sent and within the hour an express telegram came back from the client reading: 'Give Notice of Appeal immediately.'

Elaine Kellett-Bowman, MP, MEP
My husband and I both serve in the European Parliament, and, just before Christmas last year, we were attending a function in London to welcome the new French Minister and his wife.

The wife, like all good diplomats' wives, was doing her best to use the language of the host country. She looked at my husband in his pin-stripe suit, turned to me with a beaming smile, and said, 'In London I notice that all well-bred Englishmen come stripped to parties.'

David Mudd, MP

The 1964 General Election was over. The votes had been cast and counted. Labour was in. The Tories were out. The verdict of the Press: 'The Tories lost because they had become out of touch with the people.'

The headlines jarred on the former Tory MP across the breakfast table. 'Out of touch,' he muttered, 'out of touch. How can they say that I was out of touch? Damn it, man, don't these newspaper wallahs know that every Tuesday for the last twenty years I've made a point of keeping in touch by talking things over with all the chaps I've met in the grill room at the Carlton?'

Richard Needham, MP

I had rabbit on Monday,
Boiled rabbit on Tuesday,
Fried rabbit on Wednesday,
Roast rabbit on Thursday,
By Friday I had a stomach ache.
My old girl said to me, 'What you need is Castor Oil.'
I said, 'I don't, I need a ferret!'

Sir Paul Bryan, DSO, MC, MP

Conjurer, to Yorkshire yokel: 'Now, Sir, would you be

surprised if I took a rabbit out of your pocket?'
Yokel: 'I would that.'
Conjurer: 'Why would you be surprised?'
Yokel: ''Cos I've got a ruddy ferret in it.'

Sir John Hedley Greenborough, KBE

A young British diplomat, who was a bachelor, had been recently assigned to a post in a South American country. He was not a particularly sympathetic character and found it difficult to make friends amongst the other members of the Embassy staff, or indeed amongst the British community itself.

One evening the Ambassador was giving a formal ball for other members of diplomatic missions and various other dignitaries. The young bachelor was invited but found himself very much alone and therefore made an early friend of a whisky bottle.

He had partaken of quite a lot when, during one of the dances, he espied at the far end of the ballroom a beautiful svelte creature dressed in a long purple gown. He traced a somewhat unsteady path to this person and said politely, 'Will you do me the honour of dancing this Viennese waltz?'

The reply came immediately. 'There are three reasons why I will not dance with you. The first is that you have obviously had too much to drink. The second is the orchestra is not playing a Viennese waltz – it is playing the Peruvian National Anthem. And, thirdly, I am the Cardinal Archbishop of Buenos Aires.'

Keith Best, MP

A speaker at a dinner droned on at interminable length until one of the guests, seated at the end of the table, could take it no longer. He picked up an empty wine bottle, most of the contents of which he had consumed himself, and hurled it towards the speaker. Unfortunately, being somewhat inebriated, his aim was bad and rather than hitting the speaker the bottle struck the Chairman who was seated beside him. As he clutched his head and sank beneath the table the Chairman was heard to exclaim, 'Hit me again, I can still hear the swine.'

Peter Walker, PC, MBE, MP,

Winston Churchill, when Prime Minister, was approached by BOAC to allow sixty Members of Parliament to go up in a Comet airliner to obtain publicity for the Comet. The Prime Minister replied, 'I think it would be disastrous if suddenly the country were plunged into sixty by-elections, besides which, throughout my long public career I have always maintained that it is unwise to put all your baskets into one egg.'

Mrs Sheila Faith, JP, MP

Joe Bloggs, having been found guilty of theft, was being questioned by the Chairman of the Bench as to his financial situation so that an appropriate fine could be levied upon him.

After asking the usual questions about rent, rates, hire-purchase commitments, etc., the Magistrate asked, 'Do you smoke, my man?'

Joe replied, 'Thank you very much, Your Worship, it's very kind of you, but not just at the moment.'

Iain Sproat, MP

A musician with a tin whistle played right through a village in Aberdeenshire, near where I live, without getting anything for his trouble. As he passed the last door, he turned to a village inhabitant standing there. 'Man,' he said, 'I haven't got a single penny in this whole place!'

'I didn't think you would,' replied the inhabitant. 'You see, we do all our own whistling here.'

Roger Sims, MP

A young woman, possessed of extremely good looks and figure, poisoned her husband, of whom she had tired. Her crime was discovered; she was tried, convicted, and, this being in the days of capital punishment, she was sentenced to death.

On the eve of her execution she was asked if she had any last wish. Yes, she said, she wished to leave this world as she had entered it, unencumbered by clothing. There being nothing in the regulations against this, the Governor consented and next morning she appeared at her cell door and commenced her last walk in, so to speak, her natural state.

As she reached the scaffold the hangman could not help but cast admiring eyes at what he saw. 'My,' he muttered, 'that's a beautiful body you have there.'

'Yes,' came the reply, 'and it's all yours if you keep your trap shut.'

John Cope, MP, Treasurer to H.M. Household

I have changed my job from being an accountant to being a politician, and the difference is highlighted by the story of the tramp on the embankment between Westminster and the City who stopped a man and said, 'Can I have a shilling, Guv'nor? I haven't eaten for a week.' The man was a politician and said, 'Never mind, next week will be better.'

The tramp tried the same line on the next man who came along. This man was an accountant. He adjusted his glasses and asked, 'How does that compare with the same period last year?'

The Hon. Peter Morrison, MP

'Behind every successful man stands an astonished mother-in- law.'

Nicholas Edwards, PC, MP

Winston Churchill was addressing the House of Commons when a Labour Member called Paling shouted, 'You dirty dog!'

'Yes,' snapped Winston, 'and remember what dirty dogs do to palings!'

Kenneth Carlisle, MP

While at University I was asked to speak at my first political meeting. It was held in some remote and draughty village hall a few miles from the University. Apart from the Chairman, only two men, a woman and a dog were present, all seated at the back of the hall. The Chairman rose to open the meeting, and at once berated the audience, fuming, 'If more of you don't turn up we'll never get a good speaker'

David Myles, MP

In the George Orwellian situation of Animal Farm, the hen and the pig were having a discussion. 'I have great difficulty,' said the pig, 'in fully understanding some of these language terms. For instance, what is the difference between participating and being involved?'

'That's easy,' said the hen, 'you know the ham and egg breakfast enjoyed by humans? Well, I participate and you are totally involved.'

Chris Patten, MP

As you may know, Calvin Coolidge was well known for his habitual silence which he justified on one occasion by saying, 'I found out early in life that you don't have to explain something you haven't said.' These silences caused problems at dinner parties. On one occasion, a Washington society leader seated next to the President said, 'Mr President I made a bet today that I could get more than two words out of you this evening.' The President looked at her for a moment and replied, 'You lose.'

On another occasion, seated next to the brilliant and talkative Alice Roosevelt Longworth at a dinner party, even her sparkling failed to thaw him out. Eventually, Mrs Longworth, somewhat exasperated said to Coolidge, 'You must get terribly bored at all the dinners you attend.'

'Well,' replied Coolidge, 'a man must eat.'

John Browne, MP

The Archbishop of Canterbury was due to make an official visit to New York. His advisers were keen to point out the aggressive nature of American radio and press reporters. They briefed and rehearsed him constantly, to prepare him to meet this onslaught.

The Archbishop landed at John F. Kennedy Airport, New York, to be greeted by swarms of reporters. The first question was from a reporter who asked, 'Say, Bishop, what do you think of the large number of brothels on the upper east side of Manhattan?'

The Bishop (thinking rapidly for an evasive and inoffensive answer) replied, 'Are there any brothels on the upper east side of Manhattan?'

Next morning, the headlines of the New York *Times* read, 'Archbishop's first question on entering New York City: 'Are there any brothels on the upper east side of Manhattan?'

Robert Atkins, MP

Outside a village hall during a recent Election Campaign,

was a Labour poster advertising a meeting. It was headlined: 'Labour will cope'. Underneath it was scrawled: 'Next week, "How to Nail Jelly to the Ceiling"!'

Keith Best, MP

An after-dinner speaker went on at great length until, one by one, all the guests had tiptoed out of the room leaving alone the speaker and one solitary guest at the table. The speaker thought it was right that, during the course of his remarks, he should pay tribute to this one individual who had remained to listen. 'I should like to thank you so much for staying to hear me,' said the speaker, to which he received the reply: 'That's quite all right, I am the next speaker!'

Kenneth Baker, MP

When Enoch Powell reached the Pearly Gates he knocked on the door and expected admittance. After a time he heard a voice from the other side saying, 'Who dat down der?' When Enoch heard this he replied, 'Oh, don't bother!'

John Heddle, MP

Lord Justice Ackner, when replying to a toast proposed by the Hon. Member for Lichfield and Tamworth at the Tallow Chandlers Hall in the City of London recently, said, 'I don't know why barristers who earn their living speaking for others should always be in such demand as after-dinner speakers. After all, surgeons, after performing the most intricate operations in the surgery during the day, don't go home and start knitting.'

John Cope, MP, Treasurer to H.M. Household
A farmer won an enormous sum on the football pools. The local newspaper reporter came and asked him what he was going to do with the £½ million and he said, 'I think I'll just carry on farming until it's all gone!'

Dennis Walters, MBE, MP
'All this talk of pre-marital relations! I never went to bed with my wife before we were married. Did you, Bishop?'
   'I don't think so. What was her maiden name?'

John Wakeham, PC, MP
Some years ago a pioneer BBC broadcaster told of sitting next to Winston Churchill while he was giving a splendid oration to a small group. The broadcaster noticed that what appeared to be notes in Churchill's hand was only an ordinary laundry slip, and he commented on this later in private to the great statesman. 'I know,' said Sir Winston, 'but it gave confidence to my audience.'

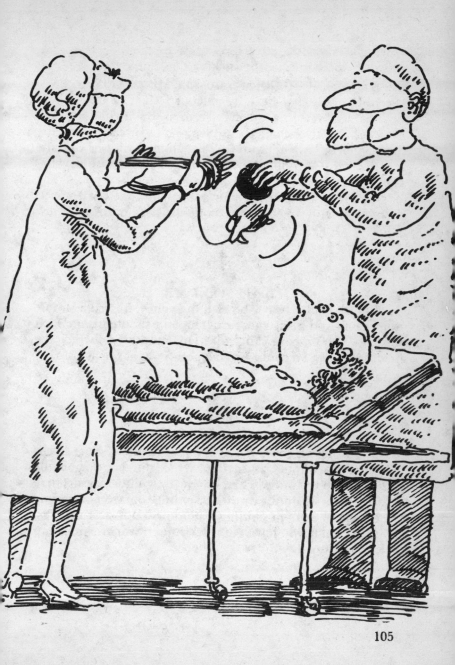

Dr Rhodes Boyson, MP

A prolific Methodist local preacher arrived at a chapel where he was to preach a special sermon by invitation. The Minister of the chapel, knowing the preacher to be long-winded, was anxious to give him a hint about the length of his sermon. 'Now tell me,' he said, 'upon what subject do you intend to speak?'

'Upon the milk of human kindness,' came the reply.

'Indeed,' said the Minister, 'condensed, I hope?'

David Madel, MP

An English fielder near The Hill in Sydney, missed a simple dolly catch and a spectator on The Hill shouted out, 'That was bad, I could have caught it in my mouth!' To which the fielder replied, 'So could I if my mouth was as big as yours.'

John Watson, MP

When passing sentence on a criminal before him, a Leeds Magistrate is quoted as saying, 'Well, this is going to be difficult. I do not know whether you are guilty or not. There is an element of doubt in this case. But you are not getting the benefit of it. I am sending you to prison for six months. If you are guilty you have got off lightly. If you are innocent, let it be a lesson to you.'

James F. Pawsey, MP

Shortly after my election I accepted an invitation to visit one of my First Schools, that is, a school catering for children aged five to eight. I was introduced by the Head Teacher to her five-year-olds as Rugby's new MP, and she asked her children what MP stood for. After some shuffling of feet a little boy put up his hand and said that he thought it stood for 'Military Police'. A little girl then volunteered her view that it stood for 'Missing Persons'. After even more shuffling of feet and hesitation a very timid little boy put his hand up and said that MP stood for 'More Pawseys'!

(James Pawsey is the proud father of 6 sons.)

Sir Dudley Smith, MP

I am a Member of Parliament and I work at the House of Commons. You probably all have your own ideas of what the House of Commons is like. It has been described to me as the only lunatic asylum in the country which is run by the inmates.

Tristan Garel-Jones, MP

A baker in Caernarvon in North Wales was known as 'Dai the Crust'. During the Investiture of the Prince of Wales he baked some special rolls to commemorate that occasion – ever since when he has been known as 'Dai the Upper Crust'!

Sir John Nott, PC, MP

Two of my constituents in Cornwall went on a package tour to Canada. As part of their trip, they were taken to see the Niagara Falls. Unfortunately, their Canadian guide belittled the size and importance of Cornwall beside the huge wealth and natural glories of Canada. On pointing out the Niagara Falls, the Canadian guide said, 'Look at that magnificent sight. You have not got anything like that back in Cornwall, have you?' To which the Cornishman replied, 'No, that's right, but we have got a couple of plumbers who could put it right!'

John Patten, MP

A midwife in a backward and mountainous part of the province, where electricity supplies were fairly rare, was attempting to deliver a baby in a dark and poorly lit room. To help matters, she asked the husband to go and get a lantern from the barn. With the aid of the additional light, she delivered a fine baby. She was clearing up afterwards when suddenly there was a bit more movement and, lo and behold, now there were twins. Shortly afterwards, the same process occurred and there were triplets. As the mother was given the fourth child to appear, she lay back exhausted and shouted at her husband, 'For heaven's sake, take that lantern away, can't you see the light is attracting them!'

Robert Atkins, MP

A strong man in a cabaret act squeezed all the juice out of a lemon and regularly challenged all comers to squeeze any more, for a £50 prize. No one ever did it, until one day an insignificant-looking chap stepped up to the stage, accepted the offer and, without trouble, squeezed at least half a cup more juice. Everyone was amazed, especially the strong man. 'Who the devil are you?' he asked. 'I am Ian ——, Chairman of the Finance Committee of the local Borough Council!'

Humphrey Atkins, PC, MP

A Royal Ulster Constabulary Police Cadet was undergoing an oral test.

INSTRUCTOR: 'You are travelling in your car down a country lane at 40 miles per hour. You pass some hooded men in a ditch who jump out, get into their car and start off after you. What would you do?'

POLICE CADET: 'Eighty!'

Eamon Kennedy, PhD, Ambassador, Irish Embassy

Although former United States President Theodore Roosevelt could shoot fast from the lip with the 'retort proper', an Irishman, who was feeling no pain at the time, once got the better of him in a Boston campaign speech exchange. Republican candidate Theodore Roosevelt was constantly interrupted by the loquacious Irishman, who

109

kept shouting, 'Me, I'm a Democrat'. Finally, Roosevelt asked the Irishman why he was a Democrat. 'My grandfather was a Democrat,' replied the Irishman, 'my father was a Democrat, and I am a Democrat.' Saracastically, Theodore Roosevelt then asked, 'My friend, let's suppose your grandfather had been a jackass, and your father had been a jackass. What would you be?'

Instantly, the Irishman replied, 'Sure, wouldn't that make me a Republican?'

Geoffrey Finsberg, MBE, MP,

An insurance agent was talking to Mr Smith whilst paying his claim in respect of his factory which had been burned down. The insurance agent said to Mr Smith, 'I notice that you increased your fire insurance on the 1st August from £10,000 to £100,000 and that your premises were burnt down on the 3rd August. Why this delay?'

Sir Paul Hawkins, TD, MP

When rabbits were a staple item of commerce in Norfolk, a baker in Thetford had such a reputation for his rabbit pies that he was getting large orders for them from the Norwich shops. One day a close friend of his complained, 'Jack, I can't make out what ha' come oover them rabbit-pies o'yours. They dorn't fare so tasty as to what they used to.'

The baker said confidentially, 'Well, y'see Jimma, tha's all a question o' what tha' Government call supply an' demand. The fac' o' the matter is, I can't git rabbits enow for all o' my customers.'

'So, what are yes a-duin' on?' asked Jimmy.

'Bor,' replied the baker in a whisper, 'atween yew an' me an' the gaatepost, I're had to fill out them pies wi' a mite o' hoss meat.'

'Blast,' said Jimmy. 'How much hoss meat d'yew reckon to put in?'

''Bout fifta-fifta,' whispered the baker, with a grin.

'What d'yew mean by fifta-fifta?' asked Jimmy suspiciously.

'Oh, one hoss, one rabbit,' said the baker.

Lord Shinwell, PC, CH

The prize in the Lincolnshire Young Farmers' raffle was a Mediterranean Cruise. The penalty for the girl who won was to keep a diary. The diary read as follows:

1st Day: Went on board ship.

2nd Day: Asked to sit at the Captain's table.

3rd Day: Went on the bridge.

4th Day: Captain makes improper sugestion.

5th Day: Captain says that if I don't he'll sink the ship.

6th Day: The day I save 866 lives.

Lord Hastings

A Minister was reading a speech blind, from a brief, not having had time to rehearse it with the personal assistant who had written it for him. All went well until he got to the peroration at the end which gave an excellent summary of the great burning question of the day and ended with the rhetorical question, 'And, what, Ladies and Gentlemen, is the answer to these great burning questions?' He turned the page and read, 'You tell 'em – I quit!'

111

David Trippier, JP, MP

On a recent Parliamentary Defence trip I had occasion to be invited into a submarine. Never having been in one before, I turned to a Chief Petty Officer and said, 'For goodness' sake, don't let me touch anything I shouldn't as this is the first time that I have been in one of these.' With a pained expression, reserved for visiting Members of Parliament, the Petty Officer said, 'In your case, sir, count the number of times we dive then add on the number of times we surface, divide by two and if there is one left over don't open that ruddy hatch.'

Lord Charteris of Amisfield, PC, GCB, GCVO, OBE

A small boy on being told by his teacher that one rabbit could reproduce itself a hundred times in a year said, 'My word, I wonder what a married rabbit could do!'

Lord McFadzean, KT

Old Scottish prayer before the Union of Parliaments:
God bless the Houses of Parliament and over-rule their deliberations to the benefit of the common people.

James Prior, PC, MP

Specifications for a 'Harmonised European'. He must have:

The Sense of humour of the German
Humility of the French
Generosity of the Swiss
Taciturnity of the Italian
Political intelligence of the Irish
Diligence of the British
(Not yet approved by the European Parliament!)

Lord Rugby

A door-to-door brush salesman arrived at a remote cottage in the country. The doorbell was answered by an elderly lady who was very reluctant to spend any money and remained impervious to all his most persuasive arguments. Finally, as she turned her back to go into her cottage, he had a sudden inspiration. Would she be interested in a lavatory brush? Although in this primitive setting it seemed highly unlikely, nevertheless he just happened to have one and it was now, as he explained, a very popular selling line. Amazingly, her interest was caught and after a little thought she bought it.

A year passed by and once more he called at the cottage. His first question naturally was about that brush. Had she found it satisfactory? 'Indeed, yes,' she replied, 'I like it very much but my husband, he's so old-fashioned you know, he still prefers toilet paper.'

Lord Charteris of Amisfield, PC, GCB, GCVO, OBE

'His knowledge of religion is limited to his belief that the Epistles were the wives of the Apostles!'

Sydney Chapman, MP

I was asked by the local press for a comment upon a recent Cabinet re-shuffle, I always knew the Prime Minister occupied the seat to the immediate south of mine, and was delighted to see that the new Chairman of the Conservative party occupied that to the north. 'Have you ever felt you're being watched?' asked the reporter. I could only repeat what my wife had said that morning at breakfast: that it was not a case of being watched, but that once again I was being overlooked.

Lord Carrington, PC, KCMG, MC

A certain very bossy and much-disliked Governor's wife at a reception one night sent the ADC to enquire the name of a tune which the band was playing, and to which she had taken a fancy.

The ADC went, and on returning she said to him, 'Captain Smith, what was the tune called?' At that moment there was a dead silence throughout the room, and in ringing and soldierly tones the ADC was heard to say, 'You will remember my kisses, Your Excellency, when I have forgotten your name.'

David Mitchell, MP

The Chairman of the County Council was waiting for a train in a country station. It arrived with two coaches which seemed to be packed, followed by two goods wagons and an empty coach. He entered the latter, and sat down, only to be joined moments later by the superintendent of a local mental asylum and fifteen of his charges. The Chairman considered his position and decided to sit tight, hoping to be left undisturbed.

The superintendent started to check the number of his charges, counting slowly; 'One, two, three, four, five, er, who are you?' he asked.

'I am the Chairman of the County Council,' replied our noble civil servant. 'Six, seven, eight ...' continued the superintendent.

Michael Latham, MP

A barrow boy was advertising his wares outside the hall in which the Labour Party were holding their annual conference. 'Buy your lucky Socialist kittens,' he shouted as he held up a small, black toy kitten for the delegates around to see. Some duly paid eighty-five pence for the mascots.

A week later, outside the same hall, the delegates were leaving the Conservative Party Conference. The same barrow boy was there, selling the same toy kittens. 'Buy your lucky Tory kittens,' he urged. Delegates paid £1 each for their mascots.

A police officer had observed all this, 'Look,' he challenged, 'I saw you last week selling exactly the same toys, but they were Socialist kittens then and no different to the Tory ones you are now selling. What on earth is going on?' 'Oh, well, Officer,' replied the barrow boy, 'the difference is that this week the kittens have got their eyes open.'

David Trippier, JP, MP

Visiting a local church on Easter Sunday, I was treated to a 'blood and thunder' sermon delivered by a visiting Welsh Minister. Half way through his sermon he hammered on the edge of the pulpit with his fist and said, '... and I say to you, if you do not repent of your sins you will surely go to Hell where there will be nothing but fornication, gambling, drinking and loose women', and a voice from the back said, 'O death, where is thy sting?' The Minister went on, 'I have in front of me two glasses, one filled with water and the other filled with gin, and in my hand I have a worm. I put the worm into the water and it swims about happily, but when I put it into the gin you can see that it has died. Now what is the simple moral of this?' ... and a voice from the back cried again. 'If you've got worms, drink gin.'

Sir David Nicolson, MEP

A mother was having breakfast with her son when he looked up from his porridge and said, 'I'm not going to school today, Mother,' to which she replied, with surprise, 'And why not?'

'I'll give you three good reason for not going. First, I don't like the boys, secondly, they don't like me, and thirdly, it's a lousy school anyway.'

At this the mother looked at him reprovingly and said, 'I'll give you two good reasons why you are going to school.

Firstly, you are forty-seven years of age, and secondly, you are the Headmaster.'

Cyril D. Townsend, MP

An unsmiling Labour Government Minister in the last Parliament solemnly told the House of Commons that he wanted 'the Monopolies Commission to have full surveillance over contraceptive sheaths, chemical fertilisers and clutch mechanisms'!

Austin Bunch, CBE, Chairman, The Electricity Council

This old boy with false legs finally took himself to Roehampton because his tin legs didn't fit at all well. The surgeon said, 'Oh dear, oh dear, we must take them both away and adjust them because they are doing you no good at all.' The old boy said, 'Well, I can't wear my spares, they are worse than these;' so the surgeon agreed to fit him up with a pair of peg legs for the interim while they repaired his proper legs, and he toddled off wering his peg legs and crutches.

This was Monday. By Friday he was very thirsty, having sat by the fire all week, and decided he would struggle down to the local; of course when he got there all his mates were very sorry for him, and by closing time he was fully loaded. They pointed him in the right direction to go home and he was all right until he got to the front gate. He knocked the gate open with one crutch and steadied himself on the path. Got his two peg legs up, lifted the other crutch, and unfortunately the first crutch slipped on a wet leaf and everything flew in every direction.

After a while the old chap sat up, reached forward and took hold of one peg leg and then the other. A look of amazement came over his face and he said, 'What a bloody silly place to leave a wheelbarrow.'

Lord Aylestone, PC, CH, CBE
A Member of Parliament thought that he would considerably improve his constituency support by asking as many questions in Parliament as the Standing Orders allowed. At the following General Election one of his election posters proudly proclaimed, 'Your sitting Member of Parliament has asked 269 Questions in the last Parliamentary Session.' Someone had scrawled underneath, 'He must be b——y ignorant.'

Mrs Reginald Eyre (Actress Anne Clements)
Lady Nancy Astor had a devastating skill at dealing with hecklers. Once, at an unruly farmers' meeting a man called out, 'Say, Missus, how many toes are there on a pig's foot?' She retorted. 'Take off your boots, man, and count for yourself.'

Tony Speller, MP
I have found great amusement in various pieces that have appeared in the press, for instance:

WANTED: Man to work on nuclear fissionable isotope molecular reactive counters and three-phase cyclotronic Uranium photo-synthesisers. No experience necessary.

Students who marry during their courses will not be

119

permitted to remain in college. Further, students who are already married must either live with their husbands or make other arrangements with the dean.

HEADLINE: NOTED GEOLOGIST STONED AT ROCK FESTIVAL

At a meeting to discuss the route of a proposed ring-road, the highways committee chairman said, 'We intend to take the road through the cemetery, provided we can get permission from the bodies concerned.'

NOTICE: BEWARE, TO TOUCH THESE WIRES IS
    INSTANT DEATH
Anyone found so doing will be prosecuted.

Alexander Pollock, MP

An old lag was in the dock in the Edinburgh Sheriff Court facing a charge of stealing a pair of trousers. To his surprise the Judge found the charge 'not proven' and told the accused that he was discharged. The man, however, seemed reluctant to leave the dock. His lawyer then urged him to go, but still he declined. 'Why ever not?' asked the lawyer. 'Because I'm wearing them now,' came the reply.

Mrs Reginald Eyre (Actress Anne Clements)

Being an actress I am very fond of stories about the theatre, and members of my profession who, even in adversity, retain a ready wit. Recently I overheard two actors talking of the proposals for the new fourth television channel; one actor thought it splendid. 'Yes,' the other agreed, 'I can see a whole new field of unemployment opening up.'

Nicholas Scott, MBE, MP
When called on as the last speaker:
'I feel rather like the No. 11 bat whose prowess was such that, as he walked out to the wicket, the horse walked over to the roller – so sure was he that the proceedings were about to come to a sudden end!'

Robert Atkins, MP
Mr Kruschev was discoursing at great length, and very critically, about the iniquities of Stalin, when a voice from the large meeting yelled, 'As one of his colleagues at the time, why didn't you stop him?'

Imagine, in Russia, under Mr Kruschev, the terrible, unbearable silence. Tension mounted, the atmosphere could be cut with a knife. Then Mr Kruschev thundered, 'Who said that?' Not a man so much as moved, let alone owned up. Then after a long, long silence Mr Kruschev said quietly, 'Now you know why!'

Nicholas Scott, MBE, MP
I feel rather like the eminent Bishop, who, when asked to respond to the Toast to the Guests after a long list of other after-dinner speakers, rose to say that he had been unsure whether a short speech (cheers!) or a lengthy speech (groan) was necessary and so he had prepared both, and would

deliver both of them (deathly hush). The short speech was 'Thank you'. The long speech was 'Thank you very much'. He sat down to deafening cheers!

The Viscount Whitelaw, PC, CH, MC, MP

To the Captain of the Royal and Ancient Golf Club: You were elected and paid to look after my interests. This you have consistently failed to do for fifteen years. Now I understand that you are to amuse yourself at my expense playing golf. I hope you lose your balls!

Robert Atkins, MP

Parliament without a Whip's Office is like a city without sewerage.

The Earl Waldegrave, KG, GCVO, TD, DL

All the economists laid end to end would reach ... no conclusion.

Roger Moate, MP

'A politician is someone who approaches every subject with an open mouth.' (*Oscar Wilde*.)

A young pupil arrived at school and said, 'I am sorry I am late, Miss, but my father got burnt this morning.'

'I am very sorry to hear that, Johnny,' she replied, 'I hope it is not serious.'

'Serious? They don't muck about up at the crematorium.'

Jim Spicer, MP

Soon after the War, Marshal Tito was invited to London and obviously given the red carpet treatment. He sailed down the Thames on a special barge with contingents of all the armed services and volunteer forces drawn up on one bank of the river. A contingent of the then Women's Volunteer Services formed part of the general parade.

Remember how strange and formidable the WVS of the wartime looked: thick lisle stockings, long skirts, hats pulled firmly down and very tight jackets. The following conversation ensued:

President Tito (through interpreter): 'And what are these?'

Pause.

'These, Sir, are the Women's Voluntary Services.'

There was a longer pause before Tito replied, 'In that case I think I would rather pay.'

Lord Carrington, CH, KCMG, MC, PC, JP, DL

A schoolboy was asked what he knew about Socrates.

He replied: 'Socrates was a Greek. He made speeches and was poisoned.'

David Heathcoat-Amory, FCA, MP

A Chinese cook was serving in a British regiment in the Second World War. He spoke very little English. One day he was badly wounded and was taken back to the field hospital.

He was put in intensive care and his bed was surrounded by life-support systems of every kind. Despite this it was obvious that he had not long to live, and the Padre was called.

The Padre approached the bed and bent over the Chinaman, who immediately took a turn for the worse and appeared to be very near death. When the Padre asked if there was any last wish or confession, the dying man frantically signalled for paper and pencil. This was quickly brought and the man scribbled some words in Chinese before he gave up the struggle and sank back dead.

The Padre was very moved by this. Clearly it contained some last message to be passed on to friends and loved ones. He reverently sent the piece of paper to be translated. When it was returned, the Padre opened it and read: 'Get your foot off the bloody oxygen pipe!'

Lord Shackleton, KG, OBE, PC

A Life Peer has a special novelty value – like a mule – no pride of ancestry and no hope of posterity.

Michael Lord, MP

While canvassing during the last General Election I came across a house with a bunch of flowers, recently delivered, on the doorstep. No one answered my knock and my energetic personal assistant, instead of popping my 'Sorry to have missed you' card through the letter box, laid it against the bunch of flowers.

The next morning a delightful note arrived for me at my campaign headquarters. It read: 'Mrs Roberts of 26, Willow Walk, is sorry she was out when you called, thank you for the lovely bunch of flowers, and will most certainly be voting Conservative.'

Neil Kinnock, PC, MP

I am repeatedly told that the greatest polar opposites can co-operate and in this business of politics it seems like useful advice. I treat the theory with some suspicion and not very long ago I was tackled by a personal manager of a major corporation, who said that he quite agreed with me on a lot of things but was exasperated by my aggressive view of the incompatibility of classes. And, after the argument had raged he said that he would prove to me how the most incompatible temperaments could get on with each other.

Whereupon he took me out to London Zoo and to a cage in which there was a great grey wolf with fangs dripping, accompanied in the cage by a sweet little spring lamb gambolling around in the corner. I was astounded, deeply impressed and I turned to him – this miracle worker – and said, 'How do you manage that?' And he told me: 'It's easy: we put a fresh lamb in twice a day.'

Malcolm Rifkind, MP

An Englishman, a Frenchman and a Russian were discussing the nationality of Adam and Eve.

The Englishman said, 'Here is a woman who gives her husband the apple, the only food she has. Only an English woman would behave in such a way.'

The Frenchman said, 'No, no, you are quite wrong. Here are a man and woman having lunch, naked in the garden. Only Frenchmen would behave in such a way.'

'No, no, comrades,' said the Russian, 'you don't know what you are talking about. Here are two people, they have no clothes to wear, hardly any food to eat and they think they are in paradise. They must be Russians.'

Sir Shuldham Redfern, KCVO, CMG

A story to demonstrate the power of the press:

There was a man in a train reading the *Daily Telegraph*. He read a page, tore it out, and threw it out of the window. He then tore out another page and threw it out of the window, and continued to do so until the man opposite, who had been watching in amazement, said: 'Why do you do that?'

'To keep away the elephants,' was the reply.

127

'But there are no elephants here.'

'You see,' said the *Telegraph* reader, tearing out yet another page and casting it out of the train window, 'it works!'

Lord Airedale

A trainer of guide-dogs for the blind remarked that people expect too much of a guide-dog, and told of a blind girl arriving with her dog in Cardiff for the first time.

She asked a lady passer-by the way to her destination. The lady bent down and said to the dog, 'You go to the third set of traffic lights, turn left and it's the second turning on the right.'

Jonathan Sayeed, MP

The directors of two leading distillers of Scotch whisky attended a funeral together. Despite being rivals in the whisky trade, for the sake of appearances, they were prepared to share a drink before the service. When one asked the other what he would have, he said he would like a whisky of his own brand; to his surprise, when buying the drinks his rival ordered the same drink for himself. To explain this seeming lack of 'patriotism', his host explained, as he passed him his glass, that he had thought it would be unseemly for them to attend a funeral with the smell of whisky on their breath.

Jeremy Hanley, MP

A lot of people believe that it must be easy being a Member

of Parliament, but it reminds me of the story of Mr Tommy Trinder who was in his Rolls-Royce in the Fulham Road when he stalled at traffic lights. He tried his best to get the car started, getting more and more flustered, but not nearly as irritated as the taxi driver who was pulled up behind him. The taxi driver started peeping his horn and got more and more animated with impatience. After about five minutes Mr Trinder got out of his car, walked back to the taxi behind him and invited the driver to wind the window down. When the driver had done so Tommy Trinder put his hand through the taxi window and banged his hand repeatedly on the horn. 'I'll tell you what,' he said, 'let's swop. I'll do this and you start the bloody car!'

Lord Ingrow, OBE, TD, JP, DL

A famous politician found only one person present at a farmers' meeting he was due to address. Wondering whether to proceed, he asked his audience, who said, 'If I only had one hen I would feed it.'

The politician thereupon delivered a complete and masterly speech, and enquired if the farmer had enjoyed it. 'Aye,' said the farmer, 'but if I'd only one hen I wouldn't have given it a bucketful.'

Ken Hargreaves, MP

Despite an excellent and varied menu in the House of Commons dining room, a Boycott curry has not yet appeared on it.

A Boycott curry is exactly the same as any other curry, but the runs take longer to come.

Lord Mancroft, KBE, TD

Early in June 1944 I happened, together with several others, to find myself on the beaches in Normandy. One afternoon, I received a message from my CO to the effect that the Corps Commander was coming along our part of the beach, to see what we were up to, and would I please straighten myself up and go and welcome the great man.

Well, it so happened that we weren't up to very much that particular afternoon. There seemed to be a lull in the proceedings and we were taking advantage of this lull to carry out a little house-keeping – humping ammunition, digging gun-pits, washing our socks, writing home to mother and taking the fuses out of those horrible Teller-mines.

In due course I ran the Corps Commander to earth. He was watching a working party under the command of our Bombardier Bean, who was leaning on a shovel, watching the Corps Commander – no saluting, or anything like that – all very *Daily Mirror* and democratic.

I was a mite embarrassed by all this nonchalance so, in a breathy stage-whisper, I said, 'What's the matter, Bombardier? Have you never seen a Lieutenant-General before?'

'Oh yes, sir,' he said, 'of course I have. But that's the first one I've ever seen standing on a live Teller-mine.'

John Corrie, MP

Canvassing as a new Member in 1964 I was in a Labour area when a very attractive young lady answered the door.

I explained who I was and she invited me in to tell her about Conservative policies. Thinking I had a 'doubtful'

and might be able to persuade her to support me, I went in and gave my long story on our policies. At this point I was offered a cup of tea which I took. I was then shown round the council house to see the problems of dampness which I might be able to help with.

Two and a half hours later after more questions and answers, I edged towards the door, content that I'd won a vote in a strong Labour area, when the lady in question said in her best Scottish accent, 'I'd better just tell you, son, that my husband is the Chairman of the local Labour party and I'm the secretary, and that's two and a half hours less canvassing you'll do this afternoon!''

Baroness Airey of Abingdon

Winston Churchill had a meeting with President Roosevelt who urgently wanted to consult him about some important matter. The President knocked on his door and entered but was rather disconcerted to see the rotund and pink form of the Prime Minister in his bath, and started hurriedly to back out in his wheelchair. Churchill said robustly: 'Come in, Mr President. England has nothing to hide from her allies.'

Roger Gale, MP

A chief executive gave an aspiring young politician a dog as a present. Their ways parted but some years later crossed again.

'How's the dog?' enquired the chief executive.

'Very depressing,' said the politician. 'When I became a councillor it would walk to heel. Then I became a committee chairman and he learned to offer his paw and shake hands. While I was Leader of the Council he would lie on his back with his paws in the air, but now that I am Mayor all he will do is sit and eat and bark!'

Lord Grade

When I was going to produce *Jesus of Nazareth* I was asked by one of the press if I could name the Twelve Apostles. I said, 'Mark, Luke, Peter and Paul', and then said, 'I can't tell you the rest of the names as I haven't finished reading the script.'

Cyril Smith, MBE, MP

Bloke in top bunk shouts out, 'Look out, I'm going to be sick.'

Bloke in bottom bunk did – and he was!

Neil Thorne, OBE, TD, MP

On the death of a lady living in a block of flats, the undertakers were called in to remove her body. On the way down the stairs, the man in front slipped, the coffin crashed to the floor, whereupon the lady sat up. Three years later she 'died' again, and when the men came to collect the body this time the husband cautioned them, asking them to avoid another terrible accident.

The Viscount St Davids

There had been a by-election in one of the great deserted

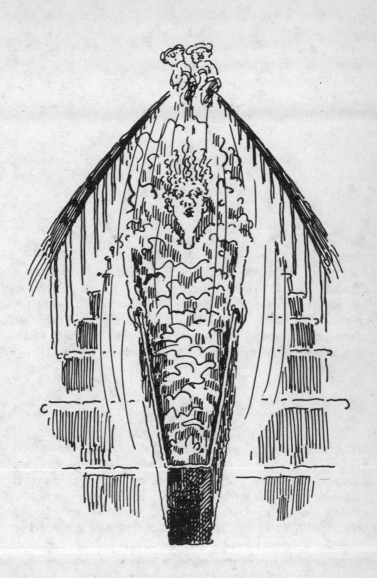

areas of the North of Scotland, and a London evening paper was commenting on the new MP.

Unfortunately they were short of space and some rather severe sub-editing had been needed.

As it finally came out, the comment read:

'The new member wears a kilt. It takes him six weeks to cover his huge constituency!'

Susan Ketelsen

On 29 November 1974, the Stretford Constituency held a Centenary Dinner to honour the memory of their MP's grandfather, Sir Winston Churchill. The Chairman was charged with proposing a toast to 'The Churchill Family'. In his speech he made much of the roles of both Baroness Churchill and Minnie Churchill and how much they had contributed towards their husbands' success; with great emphasis he further stated that behind every really great man there was a woman. The guest of honour that night was the then Leader of HM Opposition, the Rt Hon E.G.R. Heath.

Tim Sainsbury, MP

On one occasion, I was asked to speak in a debate on a Friday. The debate was delayed somewhat and things were moving rather slowly. The time was fast approaching when I had to leave to catch the train down to my constituency, so I apologised to the other speakers after making a brief contribution to the debate and hastily departed the Chamber. I sped down to the Members' Entrance to collect my coat, only to be greeted by a rather startled look from the Attendant looking at the monitor showing that I was still speaking. As I ran out of the door, a Labour Member was heard to shout, 'Don't let him out until he has finished speaking!'

Richard Hickmet, MP

I was a guest of the Turkish/Cyprus Government in August 1983 and visited that country with my wife and daughter who, at the time, was two and a half years old. We were invited to attend a lunch with the President, the Prime Minister and the rest of the Cabinet. In typical hospitable fashion our hosts insisted that we should bring our daughter as well, as the Turks love children.

We told her repeatedly that she would have to behave herself because she would be meeting the President and the Prime Minister.

The lunch went extremely well with our daughter, Sophie, crawling all over President Denktash and repeatedly asking him if he really was the President. His good humour increased on each occasion that he answered, 'Yes, I am indeed the President.'

She then turned her attentions to the Prime Minister and asked him, 'Are you the Prime Minister? Are you really the Prime Minister?' in a very sceptical voice. He too beamed and said that indeed he was. Whereupon she said, 'Oh, no, you're not. Margaret Thatcher is the Prime Minister.'

Joe Ashton, MP

When tempers were running very high during the Six Days' War between the Arabs and the Israelis there was an extremely partisan atmosphere in the House. Christopher Mayhew, the then Labour MP for Greenwich was really angry, excited and sounding off on the back benches about what the Israelis had done to the Arabs.

'The Arabs never said they would drive the Jews into the sea,' he protested. 'I will give £5,000 to anyone who can ever prove that such a statement was ever made.'

He paused for dramatic effect and a small Jewish voice cried, 'If I hear six perhaps we could do business.'

A. Cecil Walker, JP, MP

Mrs Appleby had had a tiff with her maid and fired her. The maid was packed and ready to leave, and took the opportunity to get a few things off her mind.

'It might surprise you to know that your husband thinks I'm a better cook and housekeeper than you are. He told me so himself.'

Mrs Appleby made no comment.

'And another thing, I'm better in bed than you are, too.'

'I suppose my husband told you that as well,' snapped Mrs Appleby.

'No,' said the maid, 'the chauffeur did.'

Lord Wolfenden, CBE

I had just come back from an Old Boys' Dinner at a school where I was once Headmaster. The after-dinner hours were filled by an endless stream of men, fat, bald, puce-faced, who approached me one by one with the inevitable words 'You don't remember me, sir.'

I was irresistibly reminded of a predecessor of mine who was known to be absent-minded, and deliberately played on it. When an Old Boy – any Old Boy – re-visited his school and challenged the Headmaster's memory in the traditional

way, the deliberately absent-minded old man interrupted –
'Stop! I know your name perfectly well but I *cannot*
remember your face.' He got away with that for twenty
years.

David Harris, MP

Modesty is not a characteristic normally associated with
politicians. But long before credit cards became a necessity
of life, Clem Attlee, the then Labour Prime Minister, was
having a quiet lunch in Soho of all places, with an up-and-
coming politician, the Earl of Longford. At the end of the
meal, both men found they had insufficient cash on them to
pay the bill. Longford suggested that the Prime Minister
could always pay by cheque but Attlee countered by saying,
'The trouble is I'm not known here.'

Greg Knight, MP

Members of Parliament get all sorts of problems at their
regular constituency surgeries. One young man who was in
doubt over his matrimonial intentions went to see his MP.
He unfolded his heart to his local Member and explained
that he was not sure what he should do. He needed advice
on whether he should marry a wealthy but ugly old widow
who appeared to be chasing after him or whether he should
marry the pretty – but penniless – young girl that he loved.
The MP had no hesitation in giving his advice.

MP: 'Listen to your heart, son, and take the advice it gives
you. Marry the girl you love.'

Young man: 'Yes, I am grateful. On reflection, I know that
you are right. Thank you very much. How can I ever
repay you?'

MP: 'Give me the old crow's address.'

The Earl de la Warr, DL

'No, no, a hundred times no,' said the centipede, crossing her legs.

Admiral of the Fleet Lord Hill-Norton, GCB

Before the war, when there were several hundred destroyers in the Fleet (more's the pity that there aren't today); they habitually berthed in harbour in pairs between two buoys – and a splendid sight it was to see 50 or so of them in Sliema Creek in Malta.

Hands were usually called at 0600 in those days and turned to at 0630 for an hour's work before breakfast, getting their ship bright and shiny to start the day. One summer's morning in 1935 the First Lieutenant of one V and W Class destroyer came on deck a bit early and noticed at once that his 'chummy ship' was very low in the water. It appeared that an inlet valve had failed and the resultant flooding through the night had put HMS *Nonsuch* down a good three feet in the water. He at once sent a message to his 'oppo' next door.

The early bird was still watching when the first sleepy sailors appeared on deck next door, and he had the pleasure of hearing one of them, spotting the disaster, bawl out to his mates, 'Crikey, some bugger's pinched our effing water-line.'

Nicholas R. Winterton, MP

A story told to me some years ago relates to a couple who, after a number of years of marraige, were having a typical domestic row when the husband suddenly left the room and went up to the bedroom where he began to pack. His wife, somewhat surprised, enquired as to where he intended to go and how he intended to live. He replied, in a very positive and offhand way, that he intended to go to an island he knew, where they paid 50p every time you made love. The wife casually requested further information, wanting to know how her husband expected to live on £4.50 a year.

Greg Knight, MP

One evening a policeman strolling down a dimly lit street noticed a large expensive-looking car with a House of Commons badge on the windscreen. Inside the car, the officer could see a man in the driving seat and a girl sitting alone in the back. Somewhat curious, he approached and noticed that the driver was reading a book and the young girl was sitting in the back of the car knitting. The officer opened the driver's door and asked the man what he was doing.

'Well, surely, officer, it is obvious. I am reading a book,' he intoned.

The officer was completely perplexed. 'Well, sir, what is your occupation and how old are you?' he enquired.

'I am a Member of Parliament and, if it has any relevance to the situation, I am forty-one years of age,' the MP answered.

The policeman, still none the wiser, opened the rear door

of the car and addressed the young girl, 'Well, what are you doing, miss?' he asked.

'Well, surely, you can see, officer, that I am knitting,' the pretty young thing replied.

'And how old are you, miss?' he asked.

'Well, officer, in ten minutes I will be sixteen.'

The Earl of Elgin and Kincardine, KT, JP, DL

During a visit to Cape Town some twenty years ago, my host was a Scottish bank manager. I asked him how long he had been abroad.

'Sixty years,' was his reply.

'Were you ever homesick?' I asked.

'Never,' said he, 'for you must understand I get home every other year to see my wife.'

Ivan Lawrence, QC, MP

The Lord Chancellor, Lord Hailsham (formerly Quintin Hogg) told a story at a legal dinner about a felon called Hogg who appeared before Lord Chancellor Bacon early in the seventeenth century. Hogg was found guilty and asked if there was any reason why sentence should not be passed upon him in accordance with the law. He replied, 'Yes, for I claim kinship with your Lordship.'

'How so?' demanded the great judge.

'Because,' said the felon. 'Hogg is verily akin to Bacon.'

'Quite so,' responded the Lord Chancellor, 'but only when the hog hath been well and truly hanged.'

Reg Prentice, PC, MP

A large industrial firm wanted to employ an economic adviser. They put an advertisement into the papers setting out the requirements and offering a good salary. They also specified that the successful applicant must only have one arm.

Several economists applied. They were puzzled about the one-arm requirement, but thought it must be a mistake. They were all turned down.

One of them asked: 'I have all the other requirements. Why turn me down because I have two arms?' The managing director explained that he was sick and tired of listening to advisers who said, 'On the one hand this, on the other hand that.'

Joe Ashton, MP

It is a very tense debate in the House of Commons and Willie Hamilton is accusing Harold Wilson of ratting on his commitment to the Common Market.

'First he is for the Market,' thundered Willie, 'then he is against. What does he stand for? Is he in or out? This is not the politics of leadership – it is the politics of coitus interruptus!'

There was a shocked silence, then an indignant voice called, 'Withdraw!'

Nicholas R. Winterton, MP

Cheshire has always been blessed with excellent Chief Constables, and most of them have possessed considerable skill in carrying out their difficult task, as well as a sense of humour. One such Chief Constable was presented with a set of plans for a new Police Headquarters, and asked to comment. After a lengthy study of what was a fairly complicated set of drawings, he only made one request of the architect, and that was that the urinals in the gentlemen's lavatories should be raised some six inches. When asked to justify this strange request, he merely replied that he had always sought to keep his men on their toes.

Lord Redesdale

Two tick-tack men went to the funeral of a friend in a Catholic church. As they had never been to church before they were rather nervous and sat at the back. Their consternation was complete when the priest came in and crossed himself; one tick-tack man turned to the other and said, 'I don't like the look of that, poor old Charlie's starting at 100/1!'

Robert Atkins, MP

On the day after the Election, a defeated candidate was seen walking down the street with a big grin on his face. When asked why, he said, 'If you'd seen the election promises I made, you'd be glad I lost!'

William F. Newton Dunn, MEP

The late Henry Ford I was visiting Dublin and arranged to make a donation of $5,000 towards a new local hospital. But next morning the Mayor called to apologise: 'I am sorry, sir, but the newspapers have printed that it was $50,000 and it will look very bad to have to print a correction.' Henry Ford replied by handing over a cheque for the balance, but said there would be one condition: 'There must be a plaque on the hospital wall with these words, "I was a stranger and ye took me in".'

John Mulkern, Managing Director, British Airports Authority

An Admiral and a Bishop, who loathed each other, were both in full regalia waiting for a flight from an airport during a snowstorm. The Bishop couldn't resist it: 'How long will this flight be delayed, steward', he said to the Admiral. 'Madam, if I were in your condition I wouldn't travel', came the snappy reply.

Michael Blond

Having given a particularly long and, for his audience, narcoleptic speech the night before, a pompous businessman berated his PA:

'What the hell do you think you're playing at, Smith,' he fumed. 'I asked you to write me a twenty-minute speech and the bloody thing went on for a whole hour!'

147

'But I *did* only write you a twenty-minute speech, sir,' said the puzzled PA. Then, after a moment's thought: '*And* I attached two carbon copies.'

Lord Hughes, CBE, PC, DL

Three prisoners, newly arrived at a Soviet prison camp, were talking. Prisoner number one said he had been sentenced to ten years. He could not rise in the morning and was persistently late for work; he was imprisoned for sabotaging the state's industrial effort. Prisoner number two said he also had been given ten years, but in his case he always arrived at work earlier than he had to; he was sentenced for spying for the West. When the third one was asked how long he was to be there and why, he replied that he also was in for ten years, but he was never late and never early at work. Why therefore was he there, he was asked. He replied, 'They discovered I had a Swiss watch.'

Roger Gale, MP

A Russian peasant applied to join the Communist Party. 'Are you prepared to sacrifice your house for the sake of the Party?' he was asked.

'Yes,' he replied.

'Are you prepared to sacrifice your car for the sake of the Party?' he was asked.

'Yes,' he replied.

'Are you prepared to sacrifice your wife for the sake of the Party?' he was asked.

'Yes,' he replied.

'Are you prepared to sacrifice your horse for the sake of the Party?' he was asked.

'No,' he said firmly.
'Why not?'
'Because I have a horse.'

Field-Marshal Lord Harding of Petherton, GCB, CBE, DSO
For those like Lord mayors who often have to make more than one speech on the same day:

'I am envious of the parson who said he could get away with the same sermon at morning and evening service by taking his teeth out in the morning.'

Nicholas Lyell, QC, MP

Recently, when visiting an ante-natal clinic used by my constituents, I saw on the wall a notice to young mothers about the benefits of vaccinations and other post-natal care. Above was the caption: 'Remember, the first year of life is the most dangerous.' Beneath this, someone had scrawled – 'The last is not without its hazards!'

Sir Kenneth Lewis, DL, MP

Three young drunks were apprehended by the police. They conferred together and decided to give false names, made up from names they could see when looking down the High Street.

The policeman asked the first one: 'What is your name?'

'Mark Spencer,' he said.

The second when asked said, 'Philip Sainsbury.'

The third, rather less bright, said, 'Ken Tucky Fried Chicken.'

Lord Hill of Luton, PC

Husband setting off for Masonic gathering – tarted up in glad rags. Wife, sitting quietly at home – contemplating a tired Welsh rabbit. She asks him:

'George, what would you do if you came home and found me in the arms of another man?'

His reply was instant: 'Shoot his guide-dog.'

A. Cecil Walker, JP, MP

When the Creator was making the world, he called Man aside and let him know that he was giving him twenty years of normal sex life. Man was very unhappy about this and asked the Creator for more – they were refused.

The monkey was then called, and offered twenty years. 'But I don't need twenty years,' protested the monkey. 'Ten will do.'

'May I have the extra ten years then?' pleaded Man and this time the Creator graciously agreed.

Then He called the noble lion and offered him twenty years. The lion didn't want more than ten either, so Man asked for the surplus and was granted ten more years.

Then came the donkey; he was also offered twenty years, but, as with the others, he said that ten years was ample. Man again begged for the spare ten years and got them.

This perhaps explains why man has twenty years of normal sex life, ten years of monkeying around, ten years lion about it and ten years of making an ass of himself.

Lord Grimthorpe, OBE, DL

Scene – Elderly American couple considering marriage.

Lady: 'Elmer, we have discussed everything, but what about *sex*?'
Elmer: 'My dear – infrequently, infrequently.'
Lady: 'Thank you, Elmer, but will you tell me if that is one word or two!'

The Marquess of Hertford, DL

A nonentity was boring the actress Coral Browne with a glowing description of the beauty of a much younger actress and ended up by saying 'You should have seen her when she was seventeen; her hair literally came down to her knees.'

Coral Browne smiled very sweetly and asked, 'Growing from where?'

Susan Ketelsen

In the wake of a much-publicised visit to the Stretford Constituency by the Rt Hon. Member for Down South, our MP was engaged in a walk-about in Old Trafford. A buxom West Indian lady accepted his handshake.

'And where do you live?' he enquired.
'Powell Street,' she answered.
'Oh, dear; unfortunate name, isn't it?'
'Yes, it is, but de worse ting is, me husband him called Enoch.'

The Viscount Caldecote, DSC

During the 1930s my father, then Sir Thomas Inskip, was Attorney-General, the chief law officer of the Government. One day he received the draft of a speech, to be made by His Majesty King George V, from the King's Private Secretary, with a request that he should look through it and make any comments he wished.

On reading it, my father could find nothing remotely controversial or inappropriate, and returned the speech saying he had no comments to make. But he was naturally mystified about why it had ever been sent to him.

Some time later he discovered that the King had scribbled in the margin of one paragraph a note, 'Refer to A.G.' The Secretary had assumed that 'A.G.' meant 'Attorney-General' – whereas in reality the note was to remind His Majesty, when delivering the speech, to refer to Almighty God at this point!

The Bishop of Chelmsford

The Vicar had just announced from the pulpit his forthcoming resignation. On leaving the church after the service he observed the old verger sobbing his heart out. He hastened to comfort him and said, 'You must not upset yourself, I don't doubt they will find you a new vicar as good as I am or better.'

To which the verger replied, 'I know, sir, that is what the last man said when he left, and it weren't true.'

Neil Thorne, OBE, TD, MP

Two Irishmen were engaged by British Telecom to put in telegraph poles. The foreman indicated a pile of about twenty poles at the end of one road, and showed them the marks where they were to be inserted. At the end of the day they went to collect their money and were asked by the foreman, who had been called away on other duties, how many they had planted. To his astonishment they told him three. The foreman pointed out rather curtly that his other team had planted fifteen. 'Ah,' said the first Paddy, 'but you should see how much of theirs is sticking out of the ground.'

Roger Gale, MP

A young and teetotal curate was due to give his first sermon. On the way to the church on Sunday morning he called in at the vicarage for a few words of encouragement from the boss. The vicar sat him down and, despite the young man's protests, poured him first one large glass of sherry and then a second, insisting that under the circumstances a little Dutch courage would be no bad thing.

After the service, and having delivered his maiden sermon, the young man returned to the vicarage for a de-briefing: 'Well, how did it go?' he asked.

'Not bad ... not bad at all,' said the vicar, 'but there were one or two minor errors. It was, you will now recall, the Israelites that beat the Philistines. It was not Goliath who slew David but David that slew Goliath. Oh ... and there's just one other thing. He did it with a pebble – not "a bloody great rock"!'

Lord Dean of Beswick

Commenting on the harpist in the Harcourt Room Restaurant in the House of Commons, First Peer said, 'We could do with this in the Lords.' Second Peer replied, 'Most of us have got one already, we are only waiting for the wings.'

Greg Knight, MP

Most of us, at some time or another, get accused of never admitting to our mistakes, but the biscuit is surely taken by one particular MP, who seeing someone across a crowded room, hurried over and said, 'Well, well, well, you have changed, Bill. You've lost a lot of weight, and your hair has gone all grey. I see you don't wear glasses any more and you've shaved off your beard. Crickey, Bill Jones – what on earth has happened to you?'

The man replied, 'But my name isn't Bill Jones, I'm Frederick Conway-Lyons.'

'Remarkable,' replied the MP. 'You've even changed your name.'

Lord Ironside

We solemnly go through all the business of introductions at conferences and parties nowadays and I often wonder what's in a name and why we do it, but it does cause amusement on many occasions. My name always seems to arouse interest abroad and I have always found that people cannot really understand how our parliamentary system works. Perhaps it's not surprising, when one looks at how the two Houses are constituted, that throughout my life I've always been labelled as one of Cromwell's Ironsides.

In America it conjures up an image of the USS *Constitution*, the first ironclad which was nicknamed 'Old Ironsides', so with my technology interests I have now learnt to introduce myself over there as 'New Ironsides'.

In Holland, a few years ago now, I found I was very popular suddenly and I couldn't understand why until I had to give my name at the Airport Duty Free Shop. The man behind the counter said, 'That's a very famous name. I've read about it in history.' Naturally I felt a hint of pride; the same thing happened a week later when a bright young girl said, 'That's a famous name.'

Being prepared for this, I said, 'You have seen it in the history books, I expect.'

'Oh no,' she said, 'I see him once a week on television!'

Rather deflated, I took comfort in consoling myself that the series could have been called 'A Man Called French'. After all, what's in a name?

Neil Hamilton, MP

Two Russians living in England were a bit homesick; but, because they had heard that things were a bit dodgy back in Russia, they decided that only one of them should return home and then write back about it. Before he left, the one going to Russia said, 'In case my letter is censored I'll write in black ink if things are all right and in red if they are not.'

Eventually the other chap got his letter. It was written in black ink and said, 'I am having a marvellous time in Russia. Life is wonderful and there is plenty of everything. The only thing you can't buy is red ink.'

The late Viscount Boyd of Merton, CH, DL

I once had a letter from an MP who had stumbled on the truth concerning a matter when it was not in the public's interest for me to tell him that his surmise was correct. I asked the Permanent Secretary at the Colonial Office how best it was for me to reply. He came up with –

Dear John,
I regret to inform you that your letter is not among those selected for a reply.

Tim Smith, MP

When he was Foreign Secretary in Ted Heath's Government, Sir Alex Douglas-Home (as he then was) visited Chairman Mao in Peking. He said to Mao: 'Mao, you and I are both great statesmen with a wealth of international experience. Sometimes I look back and I wonder how things might have turned out had chance played a different hand. For example,' he said, 'I wonder what would have happened if it had been Kruschev who had been assassinated and not Kennedy.'

Mao listened and thought for some time as he was wont to do. Then he said, 'Well, I don't think that Aristotle Onassis would have married Mrs Kruschev.'

Field-Marshal Lord Harding of Pertherton, GCB, CBE, DSO, MC

At one time in the Second World War carrier-pigeons were

introduced for use by forward troops to report progress in an offensive when, as happened more often than not, all telephone wires were cut by shellfire. There were no walkie-talkies or the like in those days. On one occasion everyone at a certain Divisional Headquarters engaged in an attack waited anxiously for the first pigeon to arrive. When it did the general and his senior staff officers rushed to the pigeon loft. The pigeon handler carefully removed the message and handed it at once to the general, whose face was white with dismay as he handed it to his senior staff officer, who read: 'I'm fed up with carrying this b——y bird.'

Cranley Onslow, MP

The O & M (Organisation & Methods) expert's report on Schubert's *Unfinished Symphony*:

1 The four oboe players were idle for long periods: work should be spread evenly over the whole orchestra to eliminate unprofitable peaks and troughs of activity.

2 All twelve violins appeared to be playing exactly the same tune: this represents excessive duplication. If a loud noise is really desired, it would be more economic to employ two violins and an amplifier.

3 Too much attention is given to the playing of demi-semi-quavers. All notes should be rounded up to the nearest semi-quaver. This would open the way for cost-saving through the employment of semi-skilled personnel or trainees.

4 There does not seem to be any obvious purpose in the repetition by the woodwind of a tune that has just been played by the strings. The elimination of this and other wasteful practices would reduce the length of the work by at least 15 minutes, and should have enabled the composer to finish the symphony without difficulty.

Lord King of Wartnaby

A very well known and very rich businessman was asked to address a class of students who were close to their degree graduation.

In describing his rise to fame and fortune he told them his story of how one day, when walking the streets as a penniless youngster, he became desperate to go to the lavatory.

It was a little time before he persuaded a passer-by to give him a penny.

He rushed down the steps of the public lavatory and to his great relief found a door open.

Having dealt with his problem he came back and went off and used his coin to buy some apples. He polished them up, wrapped them in tissue paper and sold them individually. He then bought some more and so on from street, to barrow, to shop, to a chain, to property and so on to his present situation.

At this point one of the students said, 'I'm sure you would like to find the man who gave you the penny.'

The speaker replied, 'I don't know about that, but I sure would like to meet the man who left the door open.'

Sir Anthony Meyer, Bt, MP

On his first parachute jump, Mick was told to jump clear of the aeroplane, count ten, and pull the rip-cord. He jumped, counted ten, and pulled. Nothing happened. As he hurtled towards the ground he saw a chap coming up equally fast towards him, with a large spanner in his hand. 'Excuse me,' he called out, 'Do you know anything about parachutes?'

'I'm afraid not,' came the answer. 'I don't know much about gas cookers, either.'

Sir Kenneth Lewis, DL, MP

Asked what the Minister's speech had been like, the new back-bencher, with engaging frankness, said: 'A bit like an ox's head; two good points and a lot of bull in between.'

Lord Cayzer

Some time ago I was reading a book entitled *The Later Cecils*, and I was struck by a legendary story which concerned Lord William Cecil, a one-time Bishop of Exeter and a man whose absent-mindedness was proverbial. On one occasion he failed to find his rail ticket when asked for it by an inspector.

'Don't trouble, my Lord,' the official assured him. 'We all know who you are.'

The Bishop replied, 'That is all very well, but without a ticket how do I know where I am supposed to be going?'

Nicholas Comfort, Daily Telegraph Political Staff

This story concerns a young farm labourer in an isolated village on the edge of the North Derbyshire coalfield, who on the outbreak of the last war was promptly conscripted down the pit. He was a strapping young lad and did well at the coal face, but from the very beginning he could not understand why he should, at the start of each shift, have to walk what seemed like miles from the bottom of the pit shaft to where he had left his pick, and the same distance back when he finished.

His second day at work, he asked the man next to him: 'Why do we have to walk miles and miles to reach the coal, and miles and miles back to the cage at night?'

'I wouldn't know about that,' said his mate. 'You'd best ask the overman.'

The next day he asked the overman the same question: 'Why do we have to walk miles and miles to reach the face, and miles and miles back to the cage at night?'

'I can't tell you that, lad,' said the overman. 'You'll have to ask the assistant manager.'

On the fourth day he met the assistant manager in the pit yard and put the question to him, his sense of waste all the greater because day by day the face was moving further away from the pit bottom.

The assistant manager could only nod sadly and say to him: 'I can't tell you that, lad. You'll have to ask the manager himself.'

The very next day, he came up from the pit bottom, having walked a few yards further even than on the fourth, to see the pit manager emerging from his ofice.

The young man walked straight up to him and asked: 'Why do we have to walk miles and miles to reach the coal face, and miles and miles back to the pit bottom at night?'

Taken aback, the manager turned to him and said: 'You can't ask questions like that. Don't you know there's a war on?'

'Oh, aye,' said the lad, whose knowledge of current affairs was limited. 'Who are we fighting?'

'Why, the Germans, of course,' said the manager.

'I'm not surprised,' replied the lad. 'We're pinching all their bloody coal.'

Lord Baker, OBE, FRS

Noah stood at the head of the gangway, running down from

the Ark, as the animals filed out, two by two. 'Go forth and multiply,' he chanted. Two snakes passed and said, rather stuffily, 'We can't, we're adders.'

A few weeks later Noah was strolling in the forest when he came to a clearing where a number of trees had been felled. To his delight he saw the snakes, surrounded by a family of little ones. 'What's this?' said he, 'I thought you couldn't multiply?' 'Well, we can't,' said the snakes, 'but we managed all right when we came across these logs.'

Nicholas R. Winterton, MP

There are many stories about the sparkling wit of that great politician and statesmen, Sir Winston Churchill. One relates to a brief meeting which he had, when he was Prime Minister, with his counterpart in the Republic of Ireland. Both countries were facing serious problems, and Churchill recalled that when he commented that, in his view, the situation in the United Kingdom was serious but not hopeless, the Irish Prime Minister replied that the situation in his country was hopeless but not serious.

Michael Stern, MP

At a very much earlier stage in my political career, I applied for selection at numerous parliamentary seats, up and down the country, most of them being held by the Labour Party with substantial majorities. Much to my surprise, my first interview was at a town in Yorkshire which was generally reckoned to be highly marginal, and, in accordance with normal practice, the Chairman of the Selection Committee wrote to me to tell me that I was required to attend for an interview of approximately half an hour but that I would not be required to make a speech, merely to answer questions.

I arrived at the constituency offices a little early, accompanied by my then girl-friend (now my wife) and shortly after we had both started work on the obligatory cups of weak tea, the previous interviewee came downstairs into the office and announced to all and sundry that he had to hurry away to get into his cricket whites. My wife claims that it was at this point she realised I had no chance whatsoever, since I could not claim to participate in Yorkshire's religion!

The Chairman invited me upstairs and as he was walking me across to a lone chair in a room which appeared otherwise packed, he invited me to make a ten-minute speech on why I thought I would be the ideal candidate for ——. Having no previous interview experience and having taken on trust his earlier letter, I do not think that I made a tremendous success of the speech although I did manage to keep going for most of the requisite ten minutes. He then called for questions and the first one was, 'Mr Stern, what can you, a foreigner from south of Doncaster, possibly have to say to the people of ——?'

Mentally at war between nerves and temper I managed to stammer out a reply, something to the effect that the problems of —— were the problems of the nation and that I was sure the electorate would find my southern accent quaint.

It was on the next question that I began to realise, like my wife before me, that the interviewing committee might not have been very interested because the second question was, 'Mr Stern, why aren't you married?' Still retaining my temper, I replied that the life of a prospective candidate could be somewhat upsetting to a family but that I did have a steady girl-friend, who I was sure would be of tremendous help in my campaign, and who had been educated in Yorkshire. The immediate supplementary question was, 'How long will she be steady?' At this point, I threw all caution to the winds and suggested that he invite her up and ask her the question himself but that I would not be responsible for the consequences. I cannot recollect any more of the interview.

The ferocity of this particular Selection Committee is perhaps evidenced by the fact that, by the time of the general election, they were on their third candidate, having already accepted and rejected two.

Neil Thorne, MP

The three biggest lies:
- Of course I'll love you as much in the morning.
- The cheque is in the post
- I'm from the Government and I am here to help you.

The three most difficult things to do:
- Write a witty after-dinner speech
- Climb a wall leaning towards you
- Kiss a woman leaning away from you.

Lord Croft

An elderly and rather absent-minded baronet was invited out to dinner. On taking leave of his host and hostess he remarked politely, 'It was very pleasant meeting you both again but I am afraid it must have been one of cook's off days and I must apologise for that.'

Jonathan Sayeed, MP

The Scots keep the Sabbath and everything else they can lay

JAQUES

their hands on.

The Welsh pray to God and on their neighbours.

The Irish don't know what they believe in, but will fight to the death to defend it.

And the English like to think of themselves as self-made men, thereby relieving the Almighty of a grave responsibility.

Anon

The President of the United States met the President of France and the Prime Minister of the UK.

'I'm in trouble,' said the President. 'I've eighteen bodyguards and one of them is a member of the KGB and I cannot find out which one it is.'

'My position is worse,' retorted the French President. 'I have eighteen mistresses. One of them she is unfaithful to me. And I cannot find out which one it is.'

'My dilemma is worst of all,' said our Prime Minister. 'I have eighteen people in my Cabinet. And one of them is quite clever ... and I cannot find out which one it is!'

Malcolm Rifkind, MP

A definition of a diplomat is one who is disarming, even if his country isn't!

Lord Aylestone, CH, CBE, PC

One evening in the late 1950s three Labour Members of Parliament spoke at a public meeting in a school hall in

Canton, Cardiff. Following the meeting and a lengthy question period, the three speakers, somewhat tired and quite hungry, decided to park the car in a side street to enjoy a hurried meal of fish and chips bought from a nearby shop.

The three speakers enjoying this succulent repast were:

James Callaghan – later to be Prime Minister.

George Thomas (now Lord Tonypandy), later to be Speaker of the House of Commons.

Bert Bowden (now Lord Aylestone), later to be Leader of the House of Commons, Lord President of the Privy Council and later still, Chairman of the Independent Broadcasting Authority.

Geoff Lawler, MP

An MP's life involves going to many dinners such as tonight's: for example, last week I was speaking at the Bradford Haemorrhoid Sufferers Society – a stand-up buffet; the week before that it was the Bolton Naturists' Group; the week before that I was invited to talk to the Idle Gay Rugby League Club Annual Dinner, and prior to that, the Eccleshill Ex-Convicts Association.

So for those of you who have heard this speech four times already this month, I apologise.

The Earl Haig, OBE, DL

An old Borderer with a good Scots accent once described an evening's fishing in the company of a friend with a wooden leg. It was nearly dark and the light was poor but the one-legged fisherman waded deeper to cover some good trout rising on the far side below a bank. Suddenly there was a tug and the fisher thought he was into a big one with that slow deliberate take that big fish are wont to make.

My Border friend described to me what happened: 'Unfortunately whote haad actually haapened was that the beesh wose a stirrk [bullock] and the flee was yoackit an ats baack – the stirrk muived yin staip, the fisherman muived as wail. Neither of them kenned whote haad haapened.' So on and on it went, the fisherman edging forward very deliberately determined not to lose the fish, and the stirk edging gradually into the darkness. The fisherman moved, the stirk moved. Again the fisherman moved, the stirk moved. This went on for some time until eventually the one-legged fisherman could wade no deeper and the 3lb breaking-strain cast was broken.

Luckily, the friend was near and able to explain what had happened, otherwise a very tall fishing story would have been told at home that night.

David Mudd, MP

Two MPs were calmly chopping an absent mutual friend to bits.

'What annoys me about him,' said the first, 'is that he has no modesty. He's a shrieking violet.'

'Yes,' agreed the other, 'he always minds his own business at the top of his voice.'

Lord Crathorne, DL

Some years ago two farmers in North Yorkshire went to court over a dispute they were having. The farmer with the

weaker case asked his solicitor if it would help if he sent the judge 'a couple of duck'. The solicitor replied that such an action would certainly lose him the case.

To the solicitor's surprise his client won the case. As soon as they were outside the courtroom the smiling farmer explained that he had in fact sent the judge a brace of duck. The solicitor was speechless with astonishment and after a short pause the farmer added, 'Aye, but I sent them in t'other man's name.'

Ken Hargreaves, MP

The person proposing a toast to the guests often finds it difficult when he knows little about them. When this happened recently to a colleague all that he knew about the chief guest was that he played golf at the local club. He rang the club to get as much information about him as he could.

'Oh, he's a war-time golfer,' said the Captain.

'What does that mean?'

'Out in 39, back in 45,' came the reply.

A. Cecil Walker, JP, MP

There was this guest speaker who was attending a function in Belfast where there were a lot of prominent politicians.

One of the problems was in giving the VIPs an opportunity to say a few words without the thing turning into a speech marathon. It was decided, therefore, to have each one of them talk for three minutes on the subject of 'Service'.

The first VIP talked about 'Service to the Public'; the next about 'Service to the Country' and so on. After more than half an hour of steady talk about 'Service', it was the guest speaker's turn to speak.

'When I was just a boy, my father had a registered bull and he was always being asked to rent the bull out for "Service" here and there. I was always curious to find out what all this "Service" was about, but my father kept putting me off, saying I was too young.

'One day my folks were in town and a neighbour sent over a message saying that he wanted to borrow the bull for a while. I figured that this would be my chance to find out what "Service" was, so I took the bull over to my neighbour.

'When I got there, the neighbour took the bull from me, thanked me for bringing him over and told me that I could go home and that he would bring the bull back himself. I told him that I wanted to stay and watch, but, just like my father, the neighbour told me I was too young.

'Well, I pretended to leave, but after a few minutes I sneaked back to the high board fence where they had taken the bull. Finally, I found a knothole. Well gentlemen, it was through that knothole in that high board fence that I saw what politicians have been doing to the people of Northern Ireland for the past fifteen years.'

John Scott

During coffee break the bank clerk heard how the milkman in his area had 'had' every woman in the street in which he lived, except one. When he confronted his wife with this news she said, 'I bet it's that miserable bitch in number 47.'

Harry Greenway, MP

Surgeon to patient after operation: 'First the bad news: we have removed the wrong leg. Next the good news: you haven't got gangrene.'

Cyril D. Townsend, MP

On one occasion the Irish writer Yeats addressed the Irish Senate on the subject of censorship. Encouraged by a crowded Chamber, he made one of the most effective speeches of his life, full of wit and wisdom, and showing a great knowledge of the religious and historical culture of his country.

When he had finished, an almost illiterate Senator stood up and said, 'Jaysus, Mr Yeats took the very words out of my mouth!'

Richard Ottaway, MP

A rather aged gentleman went into a well-established cobbler's shop in Nottingham and asked if the shoes which he had left for repair were ready.

The old man behind the counter enquired if the gentleman had a ticket, which he had, and which he handed over. It was a rather old ticket, and the man asked when the shoes had been handed in, to which the gentleman replied, 'Sometime in 1948.'

The cobbler retreated into the back room of the shop and was gone for about twenty minutes; he returned carrying a rather dusty pair of shoes and when he had blown off the dust, the gentleman said, 'Yes that's them, can I have them?'

The cobbler replied, 'They will be ready on Friday, sir.'

Greg Knight, MP

It came to pass that Neil Kinnock went to Heaven and he arrived at the Pearly Gates and said to St Peter, 'Can I come in?' whereupon St Peter said, 'Ah, now,' as he consulted a large book, 'well, according to my records, if you want to come into Heaven you are going to have to serve a penance and your penance will be to spend every night for the next three years with the lady over there, and he pointed out the most gruesome-looking creature, who looked as if she had just walked off the set of *Macbeth*. Neil Kinnock said, 'What, I can't do that, she's absolutely horrible. I'd rather go to Hell than that.' So St Peter said, 'Well, that's your choice,' and off Mr Kinnock went down to Hell. When he got there he found it occupied by Denis Healey, Harold Wilson and the Conservative Whips' Office so he decided he just couldn't take that and would rather suffer the awful penance awaiting him in Heaven.

He went back to St Peter and said, 'Now look, I have been thinking about this, can't I negotiate? Instead of all night for three years how about half a night for two years?' St Peter thought about it and said, 'Well, all right – you drive a hard bargain. The answer is yes.' Just then Neil Kinnock saw through the Gates of Heaven Anthony Wedgwood Benn walking arm in arm with Joan Collins. Neil Kinnock just couldn't believe it and said to St Peter, 'What in Heaven's name is going on; here I am the most popular Leader of the Labour Party for years, good-looking, intelligent, admired by all and there's Tony Benn, one of the most feared and divisive people in my party; how come he deserves that?' St Peter turned to him and said, 'Mr Kinnock, you just don't understand – he's Joan Collins's penance!'

Sir Kenneth Lewis, DL, MP

An Englishman in Paris was offered dinner, wine and a hostess for £25. He responded: 'The hostess can't be very good.'

Cyril D. Townsend, MP

During the time of President Idi Amin in Uganda, a judge arrived late for a banquet that was being given in a barracks by President Amin.

The short-sighted judge failed to find his name card on the table and finally plucked up courage and went over to one of the President's aides, 'Excuse me, but I cannot find my name on the table.'

The aide coolly looked up, 'Have you looked down the menu?'

Jonathan Sayeed, MP

'It's my job to talk and yours to listen. If you finish first, let me know.'

Roy Galley, MP

A mathematics teacher of mine at school uttered two lines in fairly rapid succession which became immortalised amongst us as schoolboys. On one occasion he was explaining a mathematical problem with the assistance of his blackboard and he said, 'Now watch this blackboard whilst I go through it.' This particular teacher did have some difficulty in keeping order in the class and a few days later he was heard to utter, 'Every time I open my mouth, some idiot speaks.'

The Bishop of Chichester

Dr R.R. Marett, former Rector of Exeter College, Oxford, was a great teller of tall stories. In his earlier days he had written a small pioneer work on Anthropology, published under that title by the Home University Library whose books in those days·were isued at a shilling a volume. After it was published, somebody pointed out to Dr Marett a number of inaccuracies in it, to which Marett replied, 'Huh, can't expect the truth for a shilling.'

Sir John Biggs-Davison, MP

Some of us have difficulty in remembering funny stories:

A nervous young parliamentary candidate lacked confidence as a public speaker. So he asked a senior MP of his party for advice.

'Always try to make the audience laugh *with* you,' said the latter, 'then you'll get 'em on your side.' He gave an example: 'I often start like this:

' "Some of the happiest days of my life/Have been spent in the arms of another man's wife!" Then I pause for ten seconds while the audience gapes and gasps and occasionally titters. I continue with the punch line: "I refer, of course, to my mother." '

The Candidate thanked the Member and thought he would try it at his next public meeting. He started well enough:

'Some of the happiest days of my life
Have been spent in the arms of another man's wife.'
Then the dramatic pause. He let ten seconds pass ...

fifteen … twenty seconds. The audience breathed deeply and shifted uneasily in their seats. Finally, the Candidate stammered forth: 'But I'm damned if I can remember who she was.'

Lord Cullen of Ashbourne, MBE

A well-known conductor offered to perform at a concert in a remote country village. On arriving at the rehearsal he was warned that the first violinist had got 'flu but that they had borrowed a good violinist from a neighbouring village. He was, however, warned that though a pretty good violinist, this replacement was very scruffy in appearance.

At the start of the rehearsal the conductor looked sternly at the violinist and said, 'Do you know you've got your fly buttons undone?'

The violinist replied, 'Could you hum it?'

Tim Rathbone, MP

'The trouble with political jokes is that half of them get elected.'

'Nostalgia's all right; but it's not what it was.'

Chris Patten, MP

During General de Gaulle's State Visit to Britain in the late 1950s, Lady Dorothy Macmillan was given the job of escorting the General's wife while the official talks proceeded. This was no easy task since Madame de Gaulle

was short on charm and even shorter on jolly conversation.

Day after day Lady Dorothy took Madame de Gaulle to museums, Hampton Court, and so on, without getting much of a response.

On the last day of the visit it was decided that the two ladies should go for a spin in the country to see Beachy Head. They drove down through the English countryside with Lady Dorothy's increasingly frantic efforts to get a conversation going falling on very stony ground. Eventually, they got to Beachy Head and it was a glorious afternoon. Lady Dorothy jumped from the official Humber and walked briskly to the cliff's edge. She stared into the distance and then turned and came back to the car. 'Madame,' she said, 'you must get out and see the view. It is such a clear day. I believe you can see France.' Madame de Gaulle was unimpressed. She coughed bleakly and replied, 'Je l'ai déjà vu.'

Robert Atkins, MP

Young priest to doctor: 'Why is it that talking to God is praying, but when God talks to me it's called schizophrenia?'

Ron Brown, MP

During the General Election, I regularly spoke, using a loudspeaker, outside a large Leith factory to groups of employees. This was very popular, apparently confirmed by the fact that an old lady in a nearby house kept on waving to me on each occasion.

One day, near the end of the campaign, she rushed across

the road and grabbed my arm. 'Laddie,' she said. 'I've been trying tae catch ye' for weeks – can you no' shout quietly?'

Ken Thomas, Police Constable 630A, Members' Lobby
A school teacher asked for one of her class to tell a story with a moral.

Johnny told the story of his grandfather in the trenches during the war.

'All his mates had been killed, miss. He only had five bullets, a bayonet and a bottle of scotch. Lonely and afraid, he suddenly saw ten German soldiers creeping up to his trench. Grandad drank the scotch, shot five Germans dead, leapt from the trench, charged, and bayoneted the remaining five.'

'A very brave story, John, but what is the moral?'

'Don't mess about with my Grandad when he's drunk!'

Lord Jacobson, MC
As Henry VIII said to his wife, 'I won't keep you long ...'

Hugh Dykes, MP
Letter to a Problem Page:

'Can you help me with my problem – I'm from a broken home, I suffer from an uncurable disease, my mother is an alcoholic, my father is in prison for embezzlement, my brother is a drug addict, I have a cousin in the SDP, I myself have been convicted three times for shoplifting, I have an uncle who has been doing seven years for GBH, my sister is

a notorious transvestite, and my grandfather has just been charged with indecent behaviour on a golf course.

'I am desperate and feeling suicidal, can you please, please help me. What *am* I going to do with my lousy rotten cousin who's in the SDP?'

Lord Davies of Leek, PC

My brother telephoned me one day to say his son was going to take his 'O' levels in Welsh, Woodwork and Scripture, and when I asked what all that was good for, he replied that his son would eventually like to set up as an undertaker, and all that would be very useful and good for business!

Cranley Onslow, MP

Three American clergymen discussing the question of when life begins. 'At the moment of conception,' says the Catholic. 'At the point of birth,' states the Episcopalian. 'You are both in error,' says the Rabbi. 'Life does not begin until the children leave home and the dog dies.'

Robin Corbett, MP

These 10 points from the Health Education Council booklet *Feeling Great* must be one of the best after-dinner stories … depending on the audience, of course!:

1 GET MOVING – choose activities you really enjoy.
2 Make it regular – preferably three times a week.
3 Keep it up for at least 15 minutes a time.

4 Start gently and increase the effort gradually.
5 Get family or friends to join you.
6 Keep a watch on your weight – stay slim.
7 Cut down fatty foods – especially dairy products and
   meat.
8 Steady on the sugar and sweet things.
9 Eat more fibre – like brown bread or wholemeal bread,
   fruit, cereals and potatoes.
10 GET STARTED – NOW!

Roger Gale, MP

A Lieutenant-Colonel: 'Since our arrival in this city, fifteen
of my soldiers have married local girls, fourteen of my
soldiers have become engaged to local girls …'

A voice from the audience: 'Stop while your still on top!"

Piers Merchant, MP

An illustration of the increasing dangers we, as a society,
face from jargon-ridden professions and bureaucrats!

A Durham miner was unfortunately injured in a pit
accident. He decided to sue the Coal Board and the case
went to court. The hearing became increasingly technical
and complicated, and eventually the issue revolved around
the miner's own responsibility for the accident.

The judge was a learned expert on the law of damages,
but possessed the other-worldliness reserved only for
members of his profession. He had never talked to a miner,
and was not even sure what they did down the pits. As the
trial reached a climax the bewigged judge, with his polished
cheeks and gold-rimmed glasses on the end of his nose,

186

stopped the legal argument and peered hawkishly over the bench to the litigant. Fixing him with a glassy stare, he then turned to the man's barrister and said, 'Has not your client heard of the well-known legal maxim *non profitere se fit injuria?*'

Quick as a flash the barrister, better schooled in the language of the pit villages, replied, 'M'Lud, they talk of nothing else in the pubs and clubs of County Durham.'

The pit man was no wiser, but the language of the common man reigned supreme.

Greg Knight, MP

A politician who was feeling unwell went to his doctor who gave him an examination and then said, 'I've got bad news for you. You've got three minutes to live.'

The politician was devastated – 'Can't you do anything for me?' he cried.

'Well,' the Doctor answered. 'I can boil you an egg!'

Ivan Lawrence, QC, MP

Judge Maud sitting at the Old Bailey sentenced two homosexuals who had committed an indecent act under Waterloo Bridge with these words:

'It is not the enormity of the crime itself that appalls one. It is the fact that you chose to do it under one of London's most beautiful bridges.'

Lady Eyre (actress Anne Clements)

How's this for an introduction to your after-dinner speech?

'Anyone who has never heard Sir Reginald Eyre speak before will be looking forward to hearing him. I am sure you will enjoy his debatable qualities, and find his speech as moving as the food has been.'

Follow that!

Sir Reginald Eyre, MP

During Lloyd George's premiership in 1917 two French Ministers arrived at Downing Street to see him. Wishing to show particular consideration, Mrs Lloyd George walked into the drawing room to explain in French to the visitors the reason for her husband's delayed arrival.

'Pardon, messieurs,' she said with careful diction, 'Mon mari est dans le cabinet et je crois qu'il serra longtemps parce que il a pris beaucoup de papier avec lui.'

Steve Norris, MP

An Englishman, an Irishman and a Scotsman were walking on holiday in the Vatican gardens. As they turned a corner, they saw to their horror the unmistakable figure of the Pope lying prone before them. A hastily summoned cleric confirmed the Pontiff's demise and, obviously agitated, swore the three to silence until two or three days had lapsed in which a formal announcement could be made.

Musing over the extraordinary incident on the plane

home the next day, the Englishman suddenly hit on the idea that they could make a fortune by placing a large bet on the likelihood of the Pope being pronounced dead within the next week. They all agreed it was a first-class idea and agreed to meet in a few days to compare results.

A week later the Englishman stepped out of a new Rolls-Royce to meet the Scot emerging from a brand-new Mercedes. 'Well, I shall never work again,' said the Englishman. 'I got a thousand to one and laid on a thousand pounds.' 'I didn't do badly,' said the Scotsman, 'but not being so flush I only bet a hundred pounds.' Just then, the Irishman appeared alighting from a nearby bus. 'What happened to you?' they asked. 'I lost.' 'How could you possibly lose?' 'Well,' said the Irishman, 'I thought it was such a good idea, I did him in a double with the Archbishop of Canterbury.'

Lord Lloyd, MBE, DL

The Headmaster of a well-known public school decided that it was necessary to raise the school fees. So he wrote round to parents to say that the fees would have to be raised by £x per annum. Unfortunately his secretary omitted one of the n's so that it read 'per anum'. A friend of mine on receiving this missive wrote back and said that whilst regretting the rise in the fees, he would prefer to pay through the nose as before.

Lord Croft

A recently ennobled politician was asked by a waiter at a party what his name was. Indignant at not being recognised he exclaimed – 'My good man, don't you know it?'

The waiter replied dryly, 'I am afraid not, sir, but I will make enquiries!'

Cyril Smith, MBE, MP

Mrs Thatcher passes on – knocks on Gates of Heaven but St Peter, after enquiring her name sends her down below. Some four days later there is a knock on the Gates of Heaven – St Peter goes and finds the Devil standing there. 'What do you want,' asks St Peter.

'Oh,' says the Devil, 'I've come to seek political asylum!'

John Wakeham, PC, MP

The story I remember best from my time at the Treasury was overhearing two Treasury Mandarins discussing a tricky problem; one said: 'That's OK in practice, but what's wrong with it in theory?'

Edwina Currie, MP

The problems with a lady politician all revolve around credibility. You see, if a politicians says 'yes' we know he means 'maybe'. If he says 'maybe' he probably means 'no'. But if he says 'no' then he's not a politician.

However, when a lady says 'no', we recognise that she means 'maybe'. And when she says 'maybe' she probably means 'yes'. But if she says 'yes', then she's no lady ...

– so what am I to do?

Lord Colwyn

When flying on a particularly long journey, the late Arthur Askey called one of the hostesses to ask if he could see some of the magazines.

When asked which magazine he would like to read, he replied 'The *National Geographic Magazine*, please.'

'I'm awfully sorry,' replied the hostess, 'we don't have that with us. Is there another one I can get for you instead?'

'How about *Playboy*?' said Arthur, after a little thought.

'Oh dear,' said the hostess, 'that's another one we don't have on this flight, I am sorry.'

After a short pause the hostess's curiosity got the better of her and she said, 'Tell me, sir, why did you ask for two so totally different magazines?'

'That's easy,' said Arthur, 'I really love looking at the places I'm never likely to go to.'

David Sumberg, MP

Shortly after being elected, I had to visit a well-known girls' boarding school in order to talk to them about my experience as a new Member. Because of the distance involved, I had to stay overnight at the school; dropping off to sleep that night in my lonely bed, I was much comforted by the notice over my bed which read 'Please ring the bell if you need a mistress in the night'.

Cyril D. Townsend, MP

During the premiership of Lord Salisbury a spot of trouble occurred in the Persian Gulf. The Prime Minister gave the Admiralty orders to send a gunboat and asked for the commander of the gunboat to report to him before he sailed.

During the course of his briefing the commander asked what he was to do if the natives in the area did not yield to the threat offered by the gunboat's arrival.

Lord Salisbury replied, 'Get up steam and leave.'

A few weeks later the gunboat arrived in the area, and its commander had an interview with the obdurate Sultan who said to him, 'Commander, I have patiently listened to you, you must now tell me what happens if we refuse to meet your unreasonable terms.'

The commander replied, 'Reluctantly, you will leave me with no alternative, but to carry out the second part of my orders.'

There was a pause, then the Sultan gave in.

Nicholas Baker, MP

We all know the story about the member of the House of Lords who dreamt once that he was making a speech in the House of Lords and woke up to find that he was!

David Amess, MP

The day after the election many Members took to the sunny

roads for the last time; the general idea being to drive leisurely around the constituency thanking all those who had voted for them.

It was a beautiful day as I stood in the open-top car using the loud-hailer to thank all and sundry for putting me into Parliament for the first time. The atmosphere was so euphoric that upon passing through the only upmarket farming section of the constituency I even had a word for the animals.

To one herd of cows I said very loudly and very distinctly, 'I should like to thank the cows of Bowers Gifford for voting Conservative.' The herd turned as one to peer at the disturber of the peace. Chuckling, I turned to face the road, only to see four or five very Conservative-looking ladies staring directly at me with *no* trace of amusement on their faces!

Susan Ketelsen
In 1979 the Secretary of State for Defence was about to speak at a public meeting in a by-election in Manchester, a place famed for its two football clubs. The Chairman's opening remarks were fairly brief, just indicating how fortunate we were to have a Cabinet Minister and concluded, 'Ladies and Gentleman, will you please welcome Francis Lee.' Francis Pym beamed. 'Francis Lee, former Manchester City and England forward.'

Jeremy Hanley, MP
It is always difficult to know how long to make a speech, but the best advice came from the Bishop of Southwark who in opening his sermon said that at Theological College he was

195

taught two rules about sermons. 'Preach about Christ and preach about twenty minutes.'

John Watson, MP

In early December last year I went along to speak at the Annual General Meeting of the Pateley Bridge Branch of the Conservative Party.

I mentioned to the Chairman that December seemed an unusual time for a branch to hold its AGM – most branches seek to have such meetings in October.

'We did have a meeting in October,' he replied, 'but only six people turned up so we decided to hold it again tonight with a bit of an incentive for people to come.'

'I see,' I said, 'and is that why I am your speaker tonight?'

'No, it's not. We've laid on some crisps and a meat pie.'

Lord Flowers

Crash programmes are of doubtful value. They remind me of the man who attempted to get nine women pregnant in the hope of producing one infant in one month.

Nicholas Lyell, QC, MP

At the time we married, my wife was teaching in an infant and junior school in Pimlico. In the classroom, they had a tank containing a goldfish, and one day the goldfish (as is their wont) died. This was noted by the children with much sadness and that evening after school my wife went to the local market and bought another goldfish, which she popped into the tank next morning. When the children arrived for class, one little boy saw the goldfish in the tank. He looked at it for a moment, then turned to my wife, his eyes bright with admiration. 'Hey, miss,' he said, 'you've got 'im workin' again!'

Tim Renton, MP

A true story that happened to me while canvassing in Sheffield on a hot June evening in 1970:

In Sheffield the tradition is that the front door is reserved for wakes and weddings. Candidates therefore go round to the back door. I did so and found myself looking in through the window at a burly steel-worker who was soaking himself down in the bath. Embarrassed, I looked away at his garden and saw it was full of primroses.

'I see you've got lots of primroses,' I said.

'Aye,' he commented.

'Did you know primroses were Disraeli's favourite flower?' I asked.

'Is that so?' he replied. 'In that case I'll dig the buggers up tomorrow.'

Gary Waller, MP

A chap from out of town was visiting London for the first time when he was attacked by muggers not far from the House of Commons. After knocking him about and robbing him of all his possessions, they left him bleeding and lying in the gutter.

Soon after, a Conservative MP came by and noticing the man in the gutter, crossed the street to see what was wrong.

'Goodness,' he said, 'you need help, my man!' and went away to telephone, praying that the ambulance had not been axed in the Government's spending cuts.

A moment or two later, a Labour MP came along, and likewise went to investigate. 'My God!' he said. 'Whoever did this to you needs help.'

Seconds after he had gone, a Liberal MP appeared on the scene. 'Quick!' he said. 'Tell me what the other two said to you!'

Edwina Currie, MP

This story should be told in a broad Derbyshire accent:

A woman MP is generally expected to look nice at functions, and not disgrace herself by sliding under the table. But I struck a unique problem at a farmers' dinner recently.

We were celebrating the extension of a local animal feeds mill, the owner of which laid on a splendid blow-out at the local hostelry. Conscious of the need to counteract the expansionary tendencies of my figure, I was a little careful of what I ate; no bread, no butter, no potatoes; a fruit juice instead of the locally brewed ale; no pudding. But it was as I started to put a saccharine tablet in my (black) coffee, that an old farmer sitting opposite, who had been watching me with increased suspicion, leaned across the table and protested, 'You may be my MP, Mrs Currie, but you ain't eaten anything yet that I grow!'

Lord Davies of Leek, PC

A farmer I knew was out walking when he came across a lad with a lighted lantern in his hand, who, when asked where he was going, said that he was going up the mountain to do some courting. The farmer then said that when he was a boy he didn't go courting with a lighted lantern, whereat the lad replied, 'When I see what your missus looks like, it might have been better if you had!'

Anon

The Chairman of the 1922 Committee (the committee of back-bench Tory MPs) was seated in his office recently when his secretary said the Prime Minister was on the line. All the secretary heard from him was, 'No, no, no, yes, no. Goodbye.'

'Well you certainly told her,' said the Secretary, 'but what was the "Yes"?'

'Oh,' he said, 'she just asked me if I was still listening.'

Ted Rowlands, MP

I recall the first time that I attempted to leglislate in 1966. The whole of the committee stage of the Finance Bill used to be taken on the Floor of the House and often we would sit until the middle of the night. The Labour Party was in Government, and I remember one night going into the Chamber and seeing six Opposition spokesmen, one Whip, and my Right Honourable Friend the Member for Cardiff, South and Penarth (Mr Callaghan), then Chancellor of the Exchequer. There was no one else on our side. I thought, 'This is disgraceful – where is the Government support?' So I sat and listened to the debate. I could not resist the temptation to intervene.

I intervened two or three times with growing confidence, only to be the target of more and more glum looks from the

Chancellor of the Exchequer. Eventually, a note was passed to me saying, 'What do you think you are doing?' What I was doing was self-evident – I was taking part in the great thrust of democratic debate. I wrote on the note 'Legislating' and sent it back. In a flash another note returned saying: 'Don't!'

Greg Knight, MP

An inexperienced Irishman was elected a shop steward and very soon announced to his members that, after meeting the management, he had some good news and some bad news to give to them.

'Give us the bad news first,' shouted one of the brothers.

'The bad news, my friends, is that due to the lack of orders, I have been forced to negotiate with the management a wage cut of 10%, but,' he continued, 'the good news is that I have persuaded the management to back-date this for six months.'

Peter Archer, PC, QC, MP

When the first Roman Legion came to Britain, they were marching along the Birmingham-Wolverhampton road, and had just reached Birchley Bus Garage, when a head emerged from the trees and shouted: 'Yah, one Black Countryman's worth ten Romans.'

The Commander, determined to teach the locals a lesson, immediately despatched ten men into the trees. There was the sound of body crashing against body, the noise of blows, cries of pain, and then – silence! They never saw the Romans again.

A moment later the head re-appeared. 'What did I tell

you? One Blackcountryman's worth fifty Romans.' Deciding that this had gone far enough, the Commander despatched fifty crack fighting troops after his tormentor. The noise and the cries continued longer this time. Then there was silence. No more Romans.

The head re-appeared. 'See – one Blackcountryman's worth a hundred Romans.' The honour of Imperial Rome was at stake. The Commander instructed a Centurion to take a crack unit of a hundred men, and not to return until the problem was finally settled. This time, the noise and the cries continued for quite a long time. Then there emerged from the trees a solitary Roman, battered and bleeding.

He managed to gasp, 'It was a trick. There was an ambush. There were two of them!'

Tony Speller, MP

On referring to one of his opponents in a General Election: 'Here is one who only opens his mouth to change feet.'

Richard Tracey, JP, MP

As a former broadcaster and press man I have often wondered about the origin of the public relations man. I recently discovered it:

Apparently when Moses was leading his people out of Egypt he arrived at the rather daunting barrier of the Red Sea. The screaming hordes of their pursuers were close behind. Somewhat desperately, he looked at the wide expanse of waters and said, 'If only I could hold up my arm now and call upon these waters to part ...'

A little chap who was standing next to him quickly said, 'My goodness, sir, if you could do that I could guarantee to

get you four pages in the Old Testament.'

The origins of the slick public relations operator are obviously deep.

John Lee, MP, Under-Secretary of State
for Defence Procurement

On having made it clear to his inquisitive daughters, Deborah (8) and Elspeth (6), that on no account must they go into his ministerial box, he received the plea: 'But daddy, we're only children – we won't tell the Germans the war secrets.'

John Hannam, MP

An English judge went over to Ireland to take assizes. A case was brought before him in which Paddy Murphy was accused of stealing three sheep. The evidence was clear cut and the judge summed up before despatching the jury to make its judgement. When they returned the foreman was asked for the verdict and he said, 'Not guilty M'Lud.' – The judge was horrified at this ridiculous verdict and sent them back to reconsider – which they did for an hour. On their return it was the same story, 'Not guilty, M'Lud.' The Judge then patiently explained that there was no possibility of such a travesty of justice being acceptable to him and they must reconsider the evidence again. This time the jury was out for two hours and when they returned the foreman was asked to give the verdict. In a trembling voice he said, 'Not guilty, M'Lud, so long as he returns the three sheep.'

Lord Chalfont, OBE, MC, PC

A distinguished Foreign Office official, now an equally distinguished member of the House of Lords, was, in his early days as a diplomat, officiating as Resident Clerk at the Foreign Office. The function of the Resident Clerk is to occupy a small flat in the Foreign and Commonwealth Office at night and over the weekend, and to deal with any crisis which might arise when the rest of the office is closed. In the course of one otherwise uneventful weekend, the Resident Clerk received in the early hours of Sunday morning a cable from a Middle Eastern post which contained the simple plea 'RULER HAS DIED SUDDENLY. PLEASE ADVISE.'

After pondering for a moment, the young official drafted a telegram of reply and went back to sleep. The telegram said quite simply 'HESITATE TO DOGMATISE, BUT SUGGEST BURIAL.'

Alastair Goodlad, MP

Prolix Minister, on finding public meeting sparsely attended: 'Chairman, was this meeting widely publicised?'

Chairman: 'No, Minister, but I fear that there must have been a departmental leak.'

John Fraser MP

Scene – MP at surgery.

1st Constituent: 'I'm being followed each night from work

by a spy who gets on the train at Earl's Court. What can I do?'

MP: 'I think you may be a bit paranoiac – but of course that doesn't mean that people aren't getting at you.'

1st Constituent: 'Suggest something!'

MP: 'Well, every night when you leave work buy a newspaper, fold it and tear a small hole in the fold and then use it as a spy hole to look at people on the tube. When the man following you realises he's been rumbled he will stop following you.'

1st Constituent: 'Thanks – I'll try.'

A week later –

1st Constituent: 'Thanks – I've tried it and it works.'

Two weeks later –

2nd Constituent: 'I'm being followed each night from work by a man with a spy hole in a newspaper …'

Robert Atkins, MP

Statistics prove anything. In London traffic one man is knocked down every fifteen minutes – and he's getting pretty fed up with it!

Robert Banks, MP

Some time ago I was discussing the problems Members of Parliament have in arriving at meetings on time with an eminent Italian MP.

I explained that on one occasion my wife and I were driving up to my constituency in Yorkshire for my Annual General Meeting. While I was travelling at some speed, a pheasant crossed the road. I could not avoid it and hit it full

on. I continued my journey. Some time later we were stopped by traffic lights and my wife persuaded me to check the front of the car to see what damage might have been done. To my horror I found that one headlamp had been smashed and there was blood on the wing of the car.

I then pulled into a garage and was able to obtain a replacement lamp and have it fitted to the car.

Meantime, I telephoned the Chairman of the meeting and explained my predicament. However, by dint of fast driving we arrived at the meeting in time to make my speech.

My Italian friend remarked that it must have been an awful experience for me and then asked, 'Did you ever manage to find out what happened to the peasant?'

Cyril D. Townsend, MP

An Englishman's attitude abroad is always a subject of wonder to the locals. A few years ago an English banker had the misfortune to be buried in an earthquake in Turkey.

Sensing the approach of some rescuers he called out, 'Hi, pick me out first – I'm English, dammit! We're not used to this sort of thing.'

David Mitchell, MP

While electioneering near Andover in the last General Election, I knocked on the door of a house, which was opened by an attractive young housewife, and explained that I was the Conservative candidate and thought voters liked to meet the man they were asked to vote for.

At that moment she was joined by a beautiful red setter. I leant forward, patted the dog and continued: 'Aren't you lovely, aren't you beautiful. I would like to take you home with me.' There then occurred a minor explosion from behind a curtain and the husband of the household emerged, not having appreciated that I was addressing the dog and not his wife.

The Earl Amherst
A Senior Staff Officer at British GHQ in Cairo during the Second World War was concerned at what seemed to be unnecessary delays in the delivery of signals. He asked the Signalling Sergeant; 'I am a signal. I have just come in. What happens to me now?' The Sergeant answered: 'Sorry, sir, you'll have to go out and come in again – in triplicate.'

Greg Knight, MP
Two Frenchmen, who were visiting England for a short holiday, were anxious to 'do what the British do' whilst they were enjoying their stay in the United Kingdom. Knowing that most Englishmen prefer 'a pint' they decided that they would forgo their regular tipple of wine and would instead drink pints. However, they were not familiar with the name of any English beer and weren't sure how to place their order without showing their ignorance.

On arriving in London they noticed a hoarding on the side of a hotel which read 'Drink Epsom Salts and feel younger'. That, they decided, was to be their drink. On entering the hotel, the barman was a little surprised to receive an order for two pints of Epsom Salts, but the hotel being a five-star establishment, he complied without demurring.

Some ten pints later, they both decided they'd had enough. 'Well, Pierre,' said one. 'Do you feel any younger?'

His friend replied, 'Well, I don't know about that, but I've just done a very childish thing.'

Lord Constantine of Stanmore, CBE, AE, DL

A music lover is one who when told that Raquel Welch sings in the bath, puts his ear to the keyhole.

Patrick Nicholls, MP

The Western Area Office of the Conservative Party keeps a list of speakers who are prepared to go to outlandish places at short notice. Some years ago I was anxious to extend my speaking experience, and it was suggested to me that I might go on the Western Area list. Within 48 hours they had provided me with my first engagement, which was to address a meeting in a small village in one of the remoter parts of Cornwall. I was impressed by how quickly they had provided me with my first engagement but the significance of it did not strike me at the time.

To ensure that I arrived in good time for this most important engagement I left early, but everything went wrong. I got lost and then my car broke down.

When I finally arrived, three-quarters of an hour late, I sprinted into the hall, which was packed. The Chairman had obviously been having some trouble keeping the audience in order. However, even before I had removed my coat, he was introducing me. 'Ladies and Gentlemen, he has arrived. I know how pleased you will all be to hear him. Ladies and Gentlemen, Tony Speller.'

Richard Holt, MP

Did you hear about the Irish Paddy who ran into his friend Mick, who said, 'Hallo I've not seen you for some time, where have you been?'

'In jail.'

'Goodness, what was it like?'

'Sure, Mick, it was just like being on holiday.'

Two weeks later Mick was charged with serious breach of the peace, being drunk and disorderly, and smashing shop windows. The magistrate looked at him reprovingly and said, 'For such an offence there must be a custodial sentence.'

'Does that mean jail?' asks Mick.

'Yes,' says the magistrate.

'In which case,' says Mick, 'will you make it the last week in July and the first week in August.'

Jonathan Sayeed, MP

When making a weekly walkabout in my constituency I was made to realise how firmly the famous member from whom I inherited the seat was fixed in people's minds. I knocked on one door to be greeted by a particularly deaf elderly lady with thick pebble glasses. 'Good afternoon,' I said clearly, 'I'm your local MP, Jonathan Sayeed.' 'Oh,' she replied, grasping my hand, 'Mr Benn, how nice to meet you; you don't look half as daft as they say.'

Sir Reginald Eyre, MP

An old story has it that Sir Winston Churchill was visiting a parachute factory when he absentmindedly took out a cigar. The fire officer rushed up to him saying, 'Sir Winston, you mustn't smoke.'

'Oh, don't worry, dear boy, I don't inhale.'

John Browne, MP

On a wet and windy day during the General Election of 1979, whilst accompanied by other canvassers, I knocked on the door of a house near Andover. It was about twelve noon. I was greeted by a girl dressed in a very light-weight nightdress. As she reached out of the door to shake my hand, her foot came out of the doorway and the front door closed behind her. She had no key and the heavy rain was making her nightdress progressively more 'see-through'. I lent her my overcoat and noticed a window open on the first floor. At last we managed to break into her father's garage and pull out a ladder up which I climbed to the window, on to her bed and downstairs to let her in. The steeplejack activities certainly prevented the loss of at least one voter.

Later that evening in the Andover Conservative Club, a couple at the bar asked how my day had been and I related the story only to discover that I was talking to the parents of the girl in question. On this fortunate occasion, Mother was amused!

John Butterfill, MP

A Texan tourist is visiting Dorset, driving an enormous Cadillac motor car, the type with fins at the back and what looks like rocket exhausts.

On passing through a village, he notices an elderly countryman mowing the village green with an extraordinarily ancient mowing machine which looks as though it properly belonged in the Science Museum.

The American stops his car and the two eye each other without speaking for some minutes. Eventually the old countryman can contain his curiosity no longer and pointing to the Cadillac says to the American, 'What be that you got there?'

The American replies, 'Why, this, this is just a little automobile, but say, what is that you have got there?' (pointing to the mowing machine).

'This, why, this ought-to-mow grass, but it don't.'

Michael Blond

A new MP was desperate to get some television coverage and approached all the TV stations telling them he was available to talk about absolutely anything at any time of day or night. Eventually he received a letter from a TV company asking if he could appear on a particular programme and if a fee of £50 would be acceptable. He wrote back by return: 'I accept. My cheque for £50 is enclosed.'

Sir John Biggs-Davison, MP

A small boy came up to visit London and stay with his aunt.
When he arrived at King's Cross they got into a taxi. They
were driving round the corner when the small boy said –
'What are those ladies standing on the pavement for?' The
aunt replied that they were waiting for their husbands. 'Why
not tell the boy the truth?' said the taxi-driver, 'they are
prostitutes.' The boy then asked if prostitutes have babies.
'Yes,' replied the aunt, 'where do you think taxi-drivers
come from?'

Simon Coombes, MP

A young candidate was canvassing in a rural area not far
from my constituency, and came upon a rather crusty old
farmer ploughing a field with an equally crusty old horse.

'Good afternoon, sir,' said our young candidate, 'I am
standing as the Conservative candidate in the local elections,
and am wondering if I shall have your support?'

The farmer squinted and rubbed his chin. 'Arr,' he
replied. 'Don't know 'bout that then! Me dad didn't vote,
me granddad didn't vote, and what's good enough for
them's good enough for me.'

At this point the candidate was trying desperately to keep
the conversation going. 'I am very interested in your method
of ploughing, sir. Do you prefer to use a horse, or have you
ever thought of getting a tractor?'

'Arr,' he replied. 'Don't know 'bout that then! Me dad
didn't 'ave a tractor, me granddad didn't 'ave a tractor, and
what's good enough for them's good enough for me.'

Seeing that he was clearly getting nowhere with the old

man, and noticing a light in the window of the farmer's cottage, the young candidate asked, 'Thank you very much for your time, sir. I was wondering if I could go up to your house and talk to your wife? Perhaps she might be interested in supporting my campaign?'

The old farmer got very thoughtful and rubbed his chin. 'Arrr!' he said. 'Don't know 'bout that then! Oi don't 'ave a wife.'

'Oh, I see,' said the young candidate.

'Naw ... Me dad didn't 'ave a wife, me granddad didn't 'ave a wife, and what's good enough for them's good enough for me!'

The Viscount Eccles, KCVO, PC

I took trouble with my maiden speech in the House of Commons (1943). It seemed to go well, but after I sat down Jimmy Maxton, an Independent Labour MP whom I had met at Nancy Astor's, came and gave me this advice:

'David, my boy, dinna put too much meat in your pie.'

K. Harvey Proctor, MP

I was invited to a school theatre group performance of *The Snow Queen*. I sat at the back of the room with the headmistress and the local Education Officer while the five-, six- and seven-year-old children sat crossed-legged on the floor – all but one young girl watching the production avidly. This young lady kept looking round at me throughout the entire performance and at the end, when she stood up to go back to the school classroom, she turned to me, looked up at me and said, 'I know who you are.'

'Oh, yes,' I said, 'and who do you think I am?'
'You're Flash Gordon,' she replied.

Greg Knight, MP
A left-wing feminist MP was addressing a number of her colleagues on the evils of smoking.

'I have been an MP for over five years and have never put a cigarette between my lips,' she ranted.

Overhearing this, an old boy responded, 'Madam, I have been an MP for twenty-five years and have never put one anywhere else.'

Lord Jacobson, MC
'Sit still, Johnnie,' said the teacher. But Johnnie kept on shuffling.

'What's the matter with you?' asked the teacher.

'Please, miss, I was circumcised yesterday, I cannot sit still.'

'Go to the headmaster,' said the teacher.

Ten minutes later Johnnie returned with the offending piece of his anatomy sticking out of his trousers.

'You disgusting hateful boy,' said the teacher. 'Have you seen the headmaster?'

'Yes, miss, he told me to stick it out until the lunch break.'

Lord Thomson of Fleet
A London antique dealer was very knowledgeable in his field but naive and inexperienced in other areas, for he

seldom left London and then only to travel occasionally to country auctions. He had never travelled abroad in his life. He was accustomed to having lunch every day at the same club, at the same time and with the same dealer friends.

One day a special sale came up in Paris which offered such an array of potential goods for his shop that he simply had to make the trip to Paris to bid for the objects himself. His friends wondered how in Heaven's name he would ever make out in a strange country, never having travelled before, not speaking the French language and not ever having had any experience of this kind.

When he returned from Paris they were anxious to find out how he had got on.

'Oh, I got along extremely well,' said the dealer, 'I had no trouble at all.'

His dealer friends were nonplussed. 'But you don't speak the language and you have never travelled before in a foreign country. How did you manage it?'

'Oh, there are ways and means,' the dealer said. 'I found I didn't really need to know how to *speak* French at all. For instance, I met an attractive young lady one afternoon and immediately we seemed to hit it off nicely even though she did not speak English, nor I French. After a few minutes I took my pencil and pad out of my pocket and drew a picture of a park with a bench. She caught on immediately and we went to the park and sat on a bench in the sun and watched the world go by.

Later on I took my pencil and pad out again and drew a picture of a theatre and she again caught on immediately. We walked along to a theatre and went in and enjoyed the play.

After the performance was over I took my pencil and pad again and drew a picture of a place-setting with wine glasses – she understood at once and we went to a lovely restaurant and had a most enjoyable dinner together.

But then a strange thing happened. She grabbed the pencil and pad and drew a picture of a four-poster bed.

Now how on earth do you suppose she ever figured out that I was an antique dealer?'

Cyril D. Townsend, MP
During the early days of British rule in Kenya, a European foreman in charge of a gang of Kikuyu labourers had a glass eye.

To keep his labourers working when he went off for his rather lengthy lunch each day, he took out his glass eye and left it on a post to watch over them.

Over-awed by the White Man's magic, they toiled hard in the heat of the day. But one day, one labourer, brighter than the rest, crept up behind the post and put his hat over the glass eye.

When the foreman returned he found the labourers sleeping soundly.

Sydney Chapman, MP
I was the only architect in the Commons when I lost my Birmingham seat in February 1974. I concluded my speech of thanks to my supporters, after the declaration, by saying that I could claim to be the only failed politician who could say literally: 'Ah, well, back to the drawing board.'

Archie Hamilton, MP
Man, driving home at night after an extremely good dinner, doing over 100 mph down the dual-carriageway in his new white Rover, notices that he is being followed by another white Rover.

222

Too late, he suddenly realises that the white Rover has an orange stripe down the side and a blue light on top. The siren wails.

'Will you get out of the car, sir, and blow into this bag?'

He lurches to his feet and is about to comply with the request when two cars crash into each other on the opposite carriageway. The police hurry across the road to take details.

Thinking quickly, our friend leaps into the car and drives off home at speed.

3 o'clock in the morning. He is woken by a hammering on the door, and with a splitting headache and frightful hangover goes to open it. It is the police.

'Were you stopped earlier this evening on the dual-carriageway?'

'No.'

'Well, do you mind if we inspect your car?'

'No, of course not, officer.'

On opening the garage door they see a white Rover, with an orange stripe down the side and a blue light on the top.

Lord Aylestone, PC, CH, CBE

It was said of a Cabinet Minister that he was such a good Minister that he would gladly travel from one end of the country to another 'To open an umbrella'.

Greg Knight, MP

I like the story about the MP who went away to a conference and, in the hotel foyer, he met a young lady who seemed quite keen on him. They went into the Reception and signed in as Mr and Mrs Smith for the night.

The next day the MP came downstairs, after breakfast in

bed and was presented for a bill for £500. He complained to the manager, 'Look, I have only stayed here one night.'

'Yes, sir,' the manager said, 'but your wife has been staying here for six weeks.'

'Moral: 'If you can't be good – be careful.'

Gary Waller, MP

Calling to see a farmer, a visitor could not help noticing something odd about one of the pigs. 'That's a fine lot of pigs you've got there,' he said, 'but tell me, why has that one there got a wooden leg?'

'Well,' replied the farmer, 'a month ago we had a fire. That pig rushed into the farmhouse, grabbed an extinguisher, got the fire under control, dragged my wife into the open air, and telephoned the fire brigade. When they got here, they found their job already done.'

'That's a remarkable story,' said the visitor. 'And that's a very remarkable pig! But you haven't told me why it has got a wooden leg.'

'A week after we had the fire,' explained the farmer, 'a burglar broke into the farmhouse while my wife and I were out. He bundled all our silver into a sack, and was about to ravish my daughter. Fortunately the pig heard the noise, crept up behind the intruder, hit him over the head with a vase and telephoned the police. When they arrived, the man was laid out on the floor, and all they had to do was to snap the handcuffs on and take him away.'

'That pig,' said the visitor, 'is the cleverest animal I've ever come across! But you still haven't told me why it has a wooden leg.'

'Come on now, be fair,' retorted the farmer, 'do you really think the wife and I would have had the heart to eat it all at once after everything it had done for us?'

Lord Caccia, GCMG, GCVO

A Minister on the Apple and Pear Development Council
replying to a supplementary question said that so far as the
Cox's Orange Pippin was concerned, he had recently heard
of a friend of a friend who had an idea: He was going to do
a little advertising on his own in France for that particular
apple. He would take an aeroplane across the Channel and
on it he would have individual Cox's apples with little
parachutes on them on which would be printed a message
that read: 'Every little French tart deserves an English Cox.'

John Mulkern, Managing Director,
British Airports Authority

The Personnel Officer at a certain airport has a sure-fire
method of putting recruits into the most appropriate section
of the airport. He puts each recruit on his own for 15
minutes in a room equipped with only a chair, a newspaper
and a TV set. After 15 minutes the Personnel Officer goes
into the room to make the job assignment. If the candidate
is standing at the window looking up at the sky, he is
assigned to the Airfield Operations Unit. If he is scribbling
on the walls, he is given a clerical job. If he is dismantling
the inside of the TV set, he is assigned to Engineering. If he
doesn't look up at all when the Personal Officer enters, he is
made a security guard. If he is standing on the chair shouting and waving his arms, he is made Shop Steward and, if
he cannot be found at all, he is made a Duty Officer.

Lord Chalfont, OBE, MC, PC

A distinguished American business man of somewhat advanced years, on retirement from his Board of Directors, bought a large house on the Eastern seaboard. The house was situated on a cliff-side overlooking the ocean, and one evening the old gentleman was out for his usual walk before going to bed. The evening was a very blustery one and when he ventured a little too near the brink of the cliff he lost his footing and fell over the brink. Fortunately he was able as he fell to grasp a very slender sapling which was growing out of the cliff, and arrest his fall. The old gentleman hung there for a few moments, terribly shaken, and then looking up he called out, 'Is there anybody there?'

All at once a great voice seemed to fill the whole of the firmament. It came out of the clouds and out of the sea and out of the cliff itself and it said in measured tones, 'There is always someone up here, my son. All that you need to do is to release your hold upon that small tree and you will descend safely to the shore below.'

The old gentleman considered this for a moment and looked down at the jagged rocks 200 feet below. Then he looked up again and said, 'Is there anybody *else* up there?'

Peter Sanguinetti, Director, Public Affairs, British Airports Authority

Whilst making an after-dinner speech in Strasbourg following an acrimonious debate on noise, a senior Italian official of DG X1 was interrupted by one of his political adversaries, who heckled 'Why have they introduced laws to stop helicopters flying over Rome?' The speaker's jaw fell,

227

but he was saved from an embarrassing silence by someone else who retorted 'Because they go wop wop wop'.

William F. Newton Dunn, MEP

A limerick ascribed to US President Woodrow Wilson:

My face did not make me a star:
Others are fairer by far.
But I do not mind it
Because I am behind it;
It's you who're in front feel the jar.

Sir John H. Osborn, MP

Many years ago, when I was driving from the State of Victoria to Sydney I arranged, on leaving Albury, to call on the Mayor of Holbrook, named after an uncle of mine, my name being John Holbrok Osborn.

As I passed through Albury and stopped at the traffic lights, I learned to my cost that one should keep the passenger door locked. A typical Australian 'digger' leapt into the car and asked: 'Going North, mate?'

I had really no option but to drive him a few hundred yards on his way and explain that I was going North but was stopping at Holbrook for lunch.

He agreed to leave the car at Holbrook but asked me to guarantee that if later on in the afternoon I found him walking up the Hume Highway, please to pick him up and take him on his way to Wollongong, where he was a shop convener. He was satisfied that a 'Pommy' would keep his word, and in return he agreed to give me dinner at the far end of our journey – the old town of Bowral.

Sure enough later that afternoon, there was this 'digger'

tramping along the highway. I stopped, picked him up, and we chatted merrily until, while going round a bend he suddenly said to me, 'Mate, whatever you do, don't stop.'

My reply was to the effect that I saw no reason why I should want to stop, but then I saw a beautiful blonde with a low neckline trying to change a wheel because of a flat tyre, and inevitably I started to slow down.

'Mate, what did I tell you, don't stop.'

So against my better judgement we drove on and then he said, 'Mate, do you see those two old girls with howlin' kids in their perambulators?'

I said: 'Yes.'

'You would have stopped, wouldn't you?'

I said: 'Yes.'

'And they would have parked one perambulator in front of your car and one behind your car, and you wouldn't have had the heart to send one of those kids flying out of a perambulator, would you?'

'I reluctantly replied: 'No.'

Then he said as we drove on. 'See those caravans and those men with beards over there?'

And as I drove by I duly acknowledged: 'Yes.'

'Well, you would have been stuck between those two perambulators, eyeing that Moll, and before you knew what had happened to you, your car, your money, your wallet, your passport, your clothes and your suitcase would have been taken from you, wouldn't they?'

Reluctantly I conceded that this might have been the case.

'And you would have been left sitting on the side of the highway, wouldn't you?'

And again I reluctantly admitted: 'Yes.'

'And,' he said, 'no one would have stopped for you, for after all I am proof of that as no one picked me up since I started walking from Holbrook.'

Reluctantly I agreed: 'Yes.'

Finally the 'digger' asserted: 'Then, I think you have had such a let-off, mate, that when we get to Bowral, instead of me buying you a meal you should buy me one.'

That is how, several decades ago, an Australian hitch-hiker managed to talk himself into a lift off me for several hundred miles, and then talked me into willingly agreeing to buy him a good dinner.

Cyril D. Townsend, MP

An elderly Peer was forced to attend a major debate in the House of Lords facing downwards. A colleague commiserated with him but the elderly Peer replied, 'I can assure you, Sir, I have heard some of the nicest things ever said to me in this position.'

John Cope, MP

The self-made millionaire lay on his death-bed and sent for his son. 'My boy, I've done everything I could to give you a good start in life – good school, university, and now you have qualified as a chartered accountant. But I believe a man should make his own money. Promise me you will bury all my money in my coffin with me.' The son promised, and when his father's funeral took place a few days later, just before the coffin lid was screwed down he wrote out a large cheque and put it in beside his father's body.

Lord Dean of Beswick

It is rumoured that menu changes are imminent in the Members' Dining-Room in the House of Commons – Cabinet Pudding changed for Banana Slip.

Greg Knight, MP

An MP was celebrating his 25th wedding anniversary and he gave a big party for all of his friends. However, for most of the festivities he was nowhere to be seen. Eventually a friend found him near the bar, drinking heavily and looking very morose.

'Good grief', the friend said, 'why are you looking so sad? You should be celebrating with your guests.'

The MP explained: 'On our wedding night we had a violent row, and I almost killed my wife. However, the thought that I might get twenty-five years in prison made me change my mind.'

The MP continued: 'Just think', he said to his friend, 'tonight I would have been a free man.'

Michael Stern, MP

When I was the Candidate for Derby South, I was very conscious of the fact that, not only were there two principal industries in the constituency, Rolls-Royce, manufacturing highly sophisticated civil aero-engines, and British Rail, whose engineering workshops were then engaged in developing the Advanced Passenger Train, but that these two huge organisations indulged in a certain amount of rivalry at all levels.

One of the problems with jet engines is that the turbo-fan blades can be severely damaged by hitting a bird in flight. Rolls-Royce had therefore developed a gun which was used to fire birds at the fan blades at various angles and speeds in order to test the results. Since the APT was to travel at much higher speeds than any train had travelled before in this country, British Rail thought it would be a good idea to test the effect on the train of hitting a bird at maximum speed. They therefore asked Rolls-Royce if they could borrow a gun.

The gun duly arrived with a complete set of operating instructions, and was set up: the only instruction missing was how to obtain the bird to be used for the experiment. On telephoning Rolls-Royce, the BR engineer was told that Rolls-Royce had a regular order for chickens from the local butcher, and so the bird was acquired.

The results were spectacular. Hurtling from the gun, the bird smashed into the train and went straight through the front of the engine, through the complex machinery inside, out through the back of the engine and in through the front plate of the tender, where it finally came to rest. Horrified at the vast damage they had done to one of their few prototypes, British Rail again telephoned Rolls-Royce – 'What did we do wrong?' they asked. A few moments thought from the other end of the 'phone, and then 'I trust that you did defrost the bird first!'